Riddled with Light

Riddled with Light:

Metaphor in the Poetry of W.B. Yeats

Mark Sanders

Stephen F. Austin State University Press
Nacogdoches, Texas

Stephen F. Austin State University Press
Stephen F. Austin State University Press
P.O. Box 13007, SFA Station
Nacogdoches, TX 75962-3007
sfasu.edu/sfapress
sfapress@sfasu.edu

Manufactured in China by Everbest Printing Co.
Through Four Colour Print Imports

LIBRARY OF CONGRESS IN PUBLICATION DATA
Sanders, Mark 1955—
Riddled with Light: Metaphor in the Poetry of W. B. Yeats / Mark Sanders

p. cm.
ISBN: 978-1-936205-72-1 (Cloth)
1. Poetry. 2. Irish Poetry. 3. Yeats, W. B. 4. Modern Poetry. 5. Sanders, Mark

The paper used in this book meets the requirements of ANSI/NISO Z39.48-1992 (R1997) (Permanence of Paper)

Table of Contents

Acknowledgment 7

Introduction, *by Stephen C. Behrendt* 9

Chapter 1— Yeats and Metaphor: Some Definitions and Examples 13

Chapter 2— Wandering Aengus: Yeat's Early Metaphorical Patterns 32

Chapter 3— Anima Bruta: Yeats's Metaphors of Blood and Beast 57

Chapter 4— Adam's Curse: Yeats's Metapoetics 84

Chapter 5— Yeats's Tower:
The Metaphor of the Aesthetic Intelligence 100

Chapter 6— The Metaphor of Dissolution:
Ironic Vision in Yeats's Later Poems
120

Chapter 7— High Talk: An Epilogue 140

Notes 150

Works Cited 163

Index 169

This book is for Kimberly, who has understood these lines for 22 years:

it seemed that our two natures blent
Into a sphere from youthful sympathy,
Or else, to alter Plato's parable,
Into the yolk and white of the one shell.

("Among School Children")

Acknowledgments

The work of this book began nearly thirty years ago—first as a small number of essays written during graduate school in English at Kearney State College; and, later, as a more focused study that developed into a doctoral dissertation at the University of Nebraska-Lincoln in 1989. Why did it take so long to turn the work into this book? Indeed, I have asked myself that question many times. First, I might say Yeats holds a permanent place in my thoughts and imagination; he continues to inform my critical and poetic stances, and, as these are important to me, his work was too significant to file away or keep shelved in various journals where drafts of chapters appeared. Second, I had been fortunate to have my Yeats manuscripts contracted twice previously; had it not been for the imposition of circumstances that had created, as Yeats might say, "such burdens of the mind" ("Nineteen Hundred and Nineteen"), this book would have appeared more than a decade ago. Largely, though, the study of metaphor in Yeats's poetry persists, and its critical and creative inquisition holds permanent value in modern and contemporary letters. How could I not return to it? The greatness of Yeats's work, even in today's context, seems indisputable. More indisputable is the measure of the poet's invention and the significance of his metaphorical designs. Thus, this study remains fresh and necessary, and, thus, my decision to complete it, after all this time.

I wish to thank a number of people for their early influence and encouragement: Don Welch, who gave me Yeats in the first place when I was a graduate student at Kearney State College; Linda Ray Pratt, of the University of Nebraska-Lincoln, for the seminars where our dialogues incited the original long study; and, Lee Lemon, Greg Kuzma, James McShane, and Donal Burns, co-members of the dissertation committee Linda Pratt chaired. Especial thanks to Stephen Behrendt for his excellent introduction to my study and for his continued endorsement of it.

Acknowledgment needs to be made to book artisan and artist, Charles D. Jones, Regents Professor Emeritus of Stephen F. Austin State University, whose wonderful woodcut of Yeats graces the dust jacket of this book. I much appreciate Stephen F. Austin State University's support of my scholarship activities; deep, deep appreciation to Stephen F. Austin State University Press; and much thanks to Lauren Hawkins and Troy Varvel for their work on the book's copy and design during recent stages of production.

Additional acknowledgment needs to be made to the editors of journals and publications where earlier versions of chapters appeared: *The Platte Valley Review* for "Adam's Curse: Yeat's Metapoetics" and "Yeats's Tower: The Metaphor of the Aesthetic Intelligence"; *The Arkansas Quarterly* for "The Metaphor of Dissolution: Ironic Vision in Yeats's Later Poems"; and *Hurakãn* for a portion of "Yeats and Metaphor: Some Definitions and Examples," appearing under the title of "Reinventing Poetic Metaphor." Reflections on Yeats's "Leda and the Swan," incorporated or revisited here in judiciously altered fashion, also appeared in two teaching supplements, edited by Dana Gioia, to X.J. Kennedy and Dana Gioia's *Literature* text (HarperCollins, 1995 and 1999).

—Mark Sanders, Nacogdoches, Texas
November 2013

Introduction

The perennial appeal of Yeats, whose reputation as one of the premier moderns now encompasses more than a century, owes in some respects as much to the times—modernity, broadly understood—as it does to Yeats's work itself. Particularly in the last three decades or so, as critical and theoretical schools (and their respective agendas) have risen, and in some cases fallen, the achievement of William Butler Yeats has endured against all manner of efforts to reduce it, classify it, codify it, prune and parcel it, a poetry of immense, intense energy and resilience that speaks as eloquently to the Twenty-first Century reader as it did to Yeats's contemporaries. And, as reputation studies have demonstrated again and again, not only is Yeats's "permanence" apparently very permanent indeed, it is also compelling: generations of succeeding poets have mined Yeats's intellectual and artistic riches, even as they have on occasion worked in the elder poet's shadows. The vital, flourishing Irish national literature at the beginning of the Twenty-first Century is eloquent testimony to Yeats's contribution to his national literature. If Yeats found Irish literature moribund, self-indulgent, and sentimental in all the worst senses of the words, he left it strong, healthy, craggy, and contentious. One instinctively associates Yeats's art with Irish nationalism, and some of his most recent critics have begun to examine that art through the lens of postcolonial theory and through the internationalist themes and cross-cultural dynamics that are central to that theory. At the same time, though, and in fact for more than a century, Yeats has frequently been defined in terms of what he (and his art, aesthetics, and poetics) opposes. A profoundly oppositional figure, then, he has nevertheless resisted critical and theoretical attempts to confine him within any neat frame, even an oppositional one.

Ultimately, it is the sweeping lines of Yeats's poetic and artistic achievement generally, considered as a relatively seamless whole, as a dynamic cultural and aesthetic project, rather than the particular details of any work or group of works, that both assures and ensures Yeats's permanence. At once intensely introspective and broadly "public" and nationalistic in nature, Yeats's poetry nevertheless speaks so as to cross any and all of the expected boundaries inscribed by time (history), place (nation), and incident, forging with its readers a bond of human sympathy that reminds us of the guiding ideals and principles of the Romantic movement that so profoundly influenced Yeats. Blake and Shelley, both of whom Yeats particularly admired, were adamant in their conviction of the humanizing—indeed the civilizing—power of what their age called "sympathy," or the ability of sentient and sensible individuals to get outside themselves and to feel wholly and deeply the pleasures and the pains of their fellow creatures; they dedicated their lives and their art to promulgating this doctrine, modeling for their readers in poem after poem the salutary effects of this restorative and ultimately redemptive sensitizing of the human heart and the human soul.

This same conviction animated Yeats no less than it had his visionary Romantic predecessors. Like them, he occupied himself again and again with myth and myth–making, understanding what modern psychology has demonstrated convincingly: the deep and profound influence upon human behavior of myth, and its centrality to the perennial struggle to organize human experience so as to render it both comprehensible and meaningful. Not only in his reification of Irish national myth and in his explorations of an idiosyncratic and personalized variety of mysticism, but also in his poems on seemingly ordinary, quotidian subjects, Yeats revealed an astonishing ability to "enter into" his subjects and to connect them with the lived experiences of his readers; this is one reason why that poetry remains so vibrant today, even for readers whose circumstances would seem to be in every way wholly different from Yeats's.

The key factor in Yeats's remarkable ability to engage his reader, as Mark Sanders effectively and thoroughly demonstrates in this insightful new study, is his sophisticated handling of metaphor. Yeats employs metaphor repeatedly and characteristically to define for us who (and what) the poet is, and to delineate how the Yeatsean poet relates to his audience and indeed to his society and his age. Yeats's poet figures are everywhere the representatives of their individual literary and cultural heritages, and as such they are spokespersons for their societies and their ages. In many respects they are—perhaps inevitably—figures of epic proportions: such indeed is the ennobling, enfranchising nature of Yeats's visionary art that, like epic art historically, it ennobles its audience and builds cultural pride and solidarity by disclosing and then reinforcing that audience's close relationship to the poet and to those who figure the poet. Yeats fully appreciated what Jacques Derrida would declare late in the Twentieth Century, that there is no such thing as non-metaphoric language. Like Kant's observation on the physical universe—that it is the pair of spectacles with which we are all born and which we can never remove—Derrida's view of metaphor is that it is inseparable from human experience and therefore from all human attempts to "communicate." We speak (and write) in figures, in a meta-language in which every verbal sign (or signifier) inevitably points to a multitude of potential "meanings" or signifieds. It is the inherent instability—or, perhaps more correctly, the *multi*stability—of these signifiers (and consequently of their multiple signifieds) that lends life to the poem (and to any unit of discourse, verbal or otherwise) by making any notion of "meaning" always a flexible, fluid *construct* that is the joint production of the originary artist, the responsive audience, and the constellation of culturally delimited signs in which that construction is both performed and mediated.

Working with what he understood to be the necessarily reciprocal nature of author-audience relations, Yeats developed a poetry in which metaphor delineates at the same moment both diversity (or difference) and oneness (or similitude), the infinite particular and the ineffable whole. For Yeats, metaphor is the mechanism by which the audience both receives and activates the poet's message, a message that is *mediated* by the metaphor in a fashion not unlike how we understand that alternating electric current (AC) functions. At any instant, that is, communication is taking place in both directions, with poet and audience intreracting both *on* and *in* the text of the individual poem, as well as on and in and the *uber*-text of the poet's *oeuvre* as a whole. For Yeats, metaphor performs a crucial function in addressing—and to some extent satisfying—the reader's desire for what she or he does not possess. "The human creature is not satisfied with what it has; it desires more and gains nothing," Sanders writes in his compelling discussion. Sanders shows us in convincing detail how Yeats struggled with this essentially paradoxical situation, moving from an early poetry (and poetics) of escapist wandering and searching for real or figurative island paradises to a mature poetry (and poetics) in which the paradise is to be found—indeed formulated—within the poet's own art, the construct in which all antinomies are resolved or at least set into a temporary, fragile equilibrium. If reason and instinct battle incessantly for dominance within the individual, Yeats reasons, then settling wholly within (or under the control of) either is capitulation and impotence. What lends life—vitality—is what Blake had a century earlier called the unavoidable opposition (or conflict) of Contraries, a dynamic tension in which neither pole finally dominates and whose unresolved tension consequently becomes the source of enduring wisdom and potency.

The enduring value of Mark Sanders's study lies in the extraordinary care and insight with which he reveals for us just how this intellectual and artistic development transpires in Yeats's work and how metaphor does indeed function as the fulcrum upon which Yeats balances the force of his vision. In engaging not just Yeats's poetry but also a full century of critical, theoretical, artistic, and cultural response to that poetry, Sanders shows us Yeats anew, laboring on his visionary engine to produce a profoundly metaphoric poetry and a poetics that enfranchises and empowers his audience by making that audience both a respondent and, more important, an active co-creator whose role in both the making and the performing of Yeats's art has for too long been insufficiently understood and appreciated. In setting this matter straight, Sanders does a service for us no less than for Yeats, and in the process he reminds us of the sheer, sweeping dynamism of Yeats's energetic and confrontational art.

Stephen C. Behrendt,
George Holmes Distinguished Professor of English
University of Nebraska-Lincoln

CHAPTER 1

YEATS AND METAPHOR: SOME DEFINITIONS AND EXAMPLES

In "The Intentional Fallacy," Wimsatt and Beardsley write, "Poetry is a feat of style by which a complex of meaning is handled all at once" (79). This complex results, most likely, from a deliberate exercise of the poet's imagination. Although a poet's imagination may occasionally create worthwhile "accidental" verses, a "feat of style" is not accidental. Rather, the poet most often imposes control upon the imaginative exercise. Writing is not merely a flood but the construction of a gate and channel through which imaginative, energetic impulses pass.

Potentially, the most imaginative complexity of meaning is the metaphor. In one sense, were it not for metaphor, language itself would not exist. As Jacques Derrida wrote in *Of Grammatology,* "there is no nonmetaphoric language" (67). Human imagination assigns significance to its utterances, and from this appointment arises not merely the ability to communicate and think but the cultural identities that define humankind. Language—more specifically writing—is what Derrida calls "freeplay" ("Structure" 481). "We can love this play," Derrida says, though we realize "'the play' is not 'natural'" (42). A human phenomenon, language and writing are contrary to nature. Writing is unnatural because language is unnatural, what Derrida calls "supplement" (144). He states that language

> adds only to replace. It intervenes or insinuates itself *in-the-place-of;* if it fills, it is as if one fills a void. If it represents and makes an image, it is by the anterior default of a presence . . . . As substitute, it is not

> simply added to the positivity of a presence, it produces no relief, its place is assigned in the structure by the mark of an emptiness. (145)

In the writing of poetry, the metaphor performs the task Derrida describes. However, because poetic metaphor-construction involves more than the relatively simple assignment of a word to a particular "emptiness," it is often the most difficult and most exciting of poetic manipulations. In its most elementary form, one which thrusts disparate concepts together for comparative purposes, the metaphor is language's arbiter—it defines and clarifies by virtue of distinction and similarity, it reconciles the tensions existent between antithetical concepts, it breathes life into language. The metaphorical utterance creates in the mind's eye the visible experience, touches our sense of the tangible and tactile, and awakes our ears to the symphony of language. The "death of [literature]," as Derrida claims, "undoubtedly announces . . . nothing but a death of speech" (8). Manipulation of language, on the other hand, keeps language alive; it makes literature—and poetry, especially—vital. Thus, if metaphor is on one level an arbiter, in its most complex forms it is also the most formidable inquisitor. When the poet makes metaphor, the poetry submits to murderous calculation; it succumbs to a willful violence. The process *must* happen this way.

Metaphor demands proximity. The simplest of metaphors designates equivalence between disparate concepts, and this juxtaposition is a particular violence asserted against each participating component. "Writing . . . is the carrier of death," Derrida says. "It exhausts life . . . . Writing in the metaphorical sense, natural, divine, and living writing, is venerated; it is equal in dignsity to the origin of value, to the voice of conscience as divine law, to the heart, to sentiment, and so forth" (17). A "venerated," metaphor-dictated poetry asserts itself. It is aggressive. The greatest poets accept this aesthetic willfully, if not tyrannically, for the poet is master of not just the poem but of the metaphor, too. Consequently, the poet controls, dictates, and molds the behavior of his or her poems.

One of the purposes for this study, certainly, is to understand metaphor better. How metaphor works, how it is used, seems paramount if one wishes to read, or to write, poetry; metaphor occupies virtually every part of poetic craft. Because this is so, a reasonable direction for a study on metaphor, in terms of optimal craft, is the explicit analysis of a great poet's work because, surely, a great poet must understand well the craft of metaphor-construction. Yeats, arguably, belongs to the classification of "greatest poets"; thus, his poetry becomes the example of my study on metaphor. One of modern poetry's most imaginative minds, Yeats wrote, "We make out of the quarrel with others, rhetoric, but of the quarrel with ourselves, poetry" (*Mythologies* 331). Though Yeats does not state it explicitly, the poet's quarrel with self is never finished. This is, in part, where metaphor is crucial to poetry. As Yeats says, "The desire that is satisfied is not a great desire, nor has the shoulder used all its might that an unbreakable gate has never strained" (*Mythologies* 337). The poet's imagination is one such "strained" shoulder. The "unbreakable gate," then, is the idea of a poem. Imagination, as Derrida states, "excites" us because it is "the most active of all" our "virtual faculties" (186). Imagination is "the only genius," "one of the great human powers" (Stevens 138-39); only through it can poetry be capable of saying, as Yeats put it, "I am so strange, so exotic, so different" (1: 119). Metaphor lets excitement continue; it guarantees not only the perpetuity of the poet's quarrel with self but also offers new ways to wage the battle. Metaphor provides the poet infinite invention and variety. Yeats says, "No man can do the same thing twice if he has put much mind into it" because "the new thing must employ a new set of nerves or muscles" (*Explorations* 430, 433).

Yeats's remarks are curious because he seems to make use of the same concepts and symbols frequently. However, his poems bear an undeniable freshness. In Yeats's work, we find "those images that yet / Fresh images beget" ("Byzantium")[1]. He tells us, "Pattern and rhythm are the road to open symbolism," for "pictures with patterns and rhythms of colours . . . interest us extremely" (2: 134). As Arthur Symons notes, "Without symbolism there can be no literature; indeed, not even language" (1). Furthermore, Symons says that metaphor and symbolism should be "conscious" (2). Symbolism is crucial to metaphor. Yeats wrote,

> All sounds, all colours, all forms, either because of their preordained energies or because of long association, evoke indefinable and yet precise emotions, or, as I prefer to think, call down among us certain disembodied powers, whose footsteps over our hearts we call emotions; and when sound, and colour, and form are in musical relation to one another, they become, as it were, one sound, one colour, one form, and evoke an emotion that is made out of their distinct evocation and yet is one emotion. (*Essays* 156-57)

"Distinct evocation" is necessary to poetry. Without it, the poetic moment—if we can call it that—occurs in the absence of symbol and of metaphor. If a metaphor is not the genius of imagination, an accident of speech would be better. But a poem should be as premeditated as its metaphor, much the way one plans a murder: one devises, erases, and redesigns the parts which undermine the whole structure. Much hard work is involved. In "Adam's Curse," Yeats writes,

> 'A line will take us hours maybe,
> Yet if it does not seem a moment's thought
> Our stitching and unstitching has been naught.
> Better go down upon your marrow bones
> And scrub a kitchen pavement, or break stones
> Like an old pauper in all kinds of weather;
> For to articulate sweet sounds together
> Is to work harder than all these . . . .

Granted, profitable accidents happen. A poet may write a good poem without much thought much the way a purse-snatcher occasionally discovers wealth beyond petty change. Usually, however, successful poems come from that "stitching and unstitching," that playful tyranny.

Besides careful manipulation of the poetic craft, we get a sense of what is necessary for poetry if we consider what Yeats says should be excluded from it. Selection and exclusion not only make poetry vibrant and alive, somehow the vibrancy in poetry transfers to the readers, exciting them by virtue of craft, symbol, and metaphor. Yeats wrote,

> If people accept the theory that poetry moves us because of its symbolism, what change should one look for in the manner of our poetry? A return to the way of our fathers, a casting out of descriptions of nature for the sake of nature, of the moral law for the sake of the moral law, a casting out of all anecdotes and of that brooding over scientific opinion . . . , and of that vehemence that would make us do or not do certain things . . . . (*Essays* 163)

Viktor Shklovsky, a Russian Formalist, attacks the notion that poetry is primarily imagery, as well as those poets who believe it is. He seems to agree with Yeats's notion of "a casting out of descriptions of nature for the sake of nature." Shklovsky states, in "Art as Technique," that "poetry is a special way of thinking; it is, precisely, a way of thinking in images, a way which permits what is generally called 'economy of mental effort,' a way which makes for 'a sensation of the relative ease of the process.' Aesthetic feeling is the reaction to the economy" (52). Shklovsky does not suggest art eases perception or that art is merely a matter of images. Rather, he argues that poetry makes perception difficult so that we must slow down and attend to the work carefully; he wants to broaden the concept of poetic technique. Thus, "economy of mental effort" is not absence of mental effort. The mind still strains and exerts itself, and the precision a poet brings to language economizes the effort. The result is "a sensation of . . . ease," not actually ease. Yeats asserts much the same notion in

"Adam's Curse." Shklovsky, again, says that

> art exists that one may recover the sensation of life; it exists to make one feel things, to make the stone *stony*. The purpose of art is to impart the sensation of things as they are perceived and not as they are known. The technique of art is to make objects 'unfamiliar,' to make forms difficult, to increase the *difficulty* and length of perception because the process of perception is an aesthetic end in itself and must be prolonged. *Art is a way of experiencing the artfulness of an object; the object is not important.* (55)

Perhaps Shklovsky's distinction between perception and knowledge requires further clarification, for this distinction separates the subjective and objective ways we view the world. For example, knowledge tells us that a two-by-four stud is a piece of framing wood with specific, measurable dimensions. However, perception, which is highly subjective, may view a stud lying on the ground as a snail's continent. Perception, then, is the imaginative recovery of the object. Because perception is one of the poet's tools, the poet who chooses to use imagination, to travel the "road to open symbolism," must also discover a voice or invention befitting the individual poem. Each poem should be unique. As Yeats tells us, we cannot do the same thing twice; if we accept that, we accept, too, the curse of the creative mind: finding the new thing to do. The new thing is not inevitable, though variety of technique, and variety in metaphor, will assist the poet's search. As Yeats said, we must be "always cutting out the dead wood" (*Variorum* 846). To use Shklovsky's phrase, poets should always use the "technique of defamiliarization" (59).

Defamiliarization is important for many reasons. First, according to R. H. Stacy (who, largely, quotes Shklovsky), the purpose of poetic image is not "to clarify the unknown by means of the known" but rather to defamiliarize the known (40). Furthermore, Shklovsky states that "an image is not a permanent referent for those mutable complexities of life which are revealed through it; its purpose is not to make us perceive meaning, but to create a special perception of the object—*it creates a 'vision' of the object instead of serving as a means for knowing it*" (qtd. in Stacy 40). While part of metaphor's purpose is to clarify, its greater purpose is to make what seems understood to us brand new. Defamiliarization clarifies while it simultaneously casts the subject of the metaphor into a new shape, one that is neither predictable nor commonplace. Poets who practice the art of poetic defamiliarization not only redefine the particulars of their world, they redefine in part what it is to be human. Defamiliarization increases inventive risk while it decreases that tendency in literature, as Stacy says, "to become habitualized, to settle into easy and familiar patterns" (33). Stacy also suggests that because some poets lack the imaginative drive, they become "intent on making what is unfamiliar familiar to their readers" (9). Such intent, however, is still a creative act as an effort at estrangement. The most dangerous lack of drive poets may have is when they become intent on making the familiar more familiar. However, the annihilation of habit and conformity liberates us.

Victor Erlich, making a study of Russian Formalism, wrote,

> It is this inexorable pull of routine, of habit, that the artist is called upon to counteract. By tearing the object out of its habitual context, by bringing together disparate notions, the poet gives a *coup de grace* to the verbal cliché and to stock responses attendant upon it and forces us into heightened awareness of things and their sensory texture. The act of creative deformation restores sharpness to our vision. (177)

Yeats finds in his poetry resemblance in juxtaposed estrangement. The nature of metaphor is one that sees contrary and complement simultaneously. Disparate notions or subjects are combined deliberately for their disparity, yet the metaphoric equivalence forces an imaginative linking according to implicit resemblances. The metaphorical mirror, its reflexiveness, makes us perceive that object and its reflection are somehow one another even when reason confirms they are not. Juxtaposition of oppositions both clarifies and makes exotic the components of the metaphorical pattern or sequence.

Wallace Stevens helps to explain this:

> The study of the activity of resemblance is an approach to the understanding of poetry. Poetry is a satisfying of the desire for resemblance. But poetry if it did nothing but satisfy a desire would not rise above the level of many lesser things. Its singularity is that in the act of satisfying the desire for resemblance it touches the sense of reality, it enhances the sense of reality, heightens it, intensifies it. (77)[2]

I would add to Stevens's statement that touching "the sense of reality" does not imply poetry must mirror reality. Much of the time, Yeats's vision of the world as illustrated in his poetry examines its subjects atypically. Yeats's poetry is incredibly complex because of many estranging manipulations of language. An example of estrangement is found in "The Scholars." The scholars are portrayed in terms that are both qualified and exotically unqualified for the portrait:

> Bald heads forgetful of their sins,
> Old, learned, respectable bald heads
> Edit and annotate the lines

That young men, tossing on their beds,
Rhymed out in love's despair
To flatter beauty's ignorant ear.

These are not scholars at all but personified "Bald heads." They are people, certainly, but the reductive estrangement makes them *not* people. The synecdoche, as a metaphoric device, suggests there is sufficient unlikeness between bald heads and scholars. The bald heads suggest more than just baldness. They suggest skulls. More than ironic, the scholars use their heads to think through their tasks; yet, skulls are empty and dead. Furthermore, the bald heads are "forgetful of their sins"; the ultimate forgetfulness of *sin* comes in the grave, not in old-age senility. Even the tone of the opening stanza suggests something deathly attends scholarship devoted to annotations and editing. Thus, though alive, the scholars are dead to life. Their Lethean sin makes theirs a damnable existence; it lacks the life and vitality of those "young men, tossing on their beds." Implicitly, that the dead can forget the lust of their youth we can forgive; what the scholars do is less forgiveable. Another estranging metaphor is found in the second stanza: "all cough in ink." On one level, the scholars' phlegm is ink. On another, the annotations and editing marks themselves are coughings, not inkmarks. From this metaphor, we get an increased feeling for the frailty, the impotence, and the grotesqueness of scholarly life and work.

The purpose of estrangement in this example is to create disturbance of emotions. The image of the scholars made less than human, and their tasks less than important, does not evoke the reader's sympathy; rather, the sensation of revulsion is activated. The scholars are estranged from their real humanity, just as the reader is estranged from the conventional perception of the scholars. The importance of any estrangement is founded upon how it affects our responsiveness to a poem, how it unsettles our trained "set of nerves" by its nerve and nervousness.

Because the metaphor, as Jakobson explains, "deals with problems of verbal structure" (3: 18), it includes much more than the traditional structure of I. A. Richards's *tenor* and *vehicle*. Granted, the combination of disparate elements is essential, but that in itself is oversimplification of the craft of metaphor. Metaphor as estrangement incorporates combining the poetic utterance to such diverse elements as grammar, sound, poetic form, and rhythm. "Verbal art" combined with "verbal structure" is what Jakobson calls "the insight of an artist and analyst combined" (3: 15). Consequently, a good poet must be both artist and analyst, for the poet designs the "verbal structure."

Beyond that, however, poetry should be what Nietzsche called a "mobile army of metaphors" (5). Thus, we return to the violence evoked by Derrida earlier in this chapter. A good poet wreaks violence upon habitual, uninventive, apoetic poetic sensibilities. When those tendencies are destroyed, a liberating play ensues. Metaphorical playfulness provides opportunity for infinite creativity. The poet may combine and select endlessly. Actively working out the possibilities makes the "army" mobile, creating in the poetry a sensation of that mobility. In the simplest definition, the metaphor is nothing more than the relationship of a subject to something located in a predicate. For example, "Dog is man's best friend." However, as Jakobson tells us,

> Besides the direct awareness of the identity between sign and object (*A* is *A*1), there is a necessity for the direct awareness of the inadequacy of that identity (*A* is not *A*1) . . . . Without contradiction there is no mobility of concepts, no mobility of signs, and the relationship between concept and sign becomes automatized. Activity comes to a halt, and the awareness of reality dies out. (3: 750)

Contradiction is necessary. Without it, metaphor cannot occur.

Paul Ricoeur takes this idea a step further. He says,

> The predicative assimilation involves . . . a kind of specific kind of tension which is not so much between a subject and a predicate as between semantic incongruence and congruence. The insight into likeness is the perception of the conflict between the previous incompatibility and the new compatibility. 'Remoteness' is preserved within 'proximity.' To see *the like* is to see the same in spite of, and through, the different. This tension between sameness and difference characterizes the logical structure of likeness. Imagination, accordingly, is the *ability* to produce new kinds of assimilation and to produce them not *above* the differences, as in the concept, but in spite of and through the differences. (146)

What Ricoeur calls "semantic incongruence and congruence," Hopkins called "comparison for likeness" and "comparison for unlikeness" (106). Kenneth Burke called it "perspectives by incongruity" (94). Keeping these notions in mind, the poet can make at least four metaphorical combinations. These are:

1. real object signified in familiar terms;
2. real object signified in unfamiliar terms;
3. unfamiliar object signified in familiar terms; and,
4. unfamiliar object signified in unfamiliar terms.

The first does little for a poem; the reader has nothing to respond to other than the "automatized" explanation of the obvious. The second and the third are the most useful. As Ricoeur stated, these "see *the like* . . . in spite of, and through, the differences." The fourth, because it does not create what Jakobson calls "contrariety" (3: 630), is subordinate to the second and third. Though exotic, the tension is simply not as intense.

In his essay, "What Metaphors Mean," Donald Davidson wrote that "metaphor is the dreamwork of language and, like all dreamwork, its interpretation reflects as much on the interpreter as on the originator . . . . Understanding a metaphor is as much a creative endeavor as making a metaphor, and as little guided by rules" (29). The fourth example noted above, under Derrida's terms, poses interpretive obstacles: the unfamiliar signified in the unfamiliar obscures. Poets who use this obscuring metaphor resort too often to private imagery, and this can be as detrimental as the self-explanatory metaphor. This notion may cause Yeats's readers trouble; however, part of the pleasure of reading Yeats's work is solving his poetic riddles; these activate or captivate the reader's imagination, and the solutions, I believe, are often found in Yeats's metaphors. Wayne C. Booth would say that "good metaphors . . . are *active*, lending the energy of animated things to whatever is less energetic or more abstract" (55).

Ricoeur states, "The *maker* of metaphors is this craftsman with verbal skill *who*, from an inconsistent utterance for a literal interpretation, draws significant utterance for a new interpretation which deserves to be called metaphorical because it generates the metaphor not only as deviant but as acceptable"; furthermore, "the utterance 'makes sense' as a whole" (144). Additionally, metaphor, according to Douglas Berggren, is "the ability to entertain two different points of view at the same time" (qtd. in Ricoeur 152). From any one of several considerations, then, the poet may *make* a metaphor.

One such place is in the rhythm of a poem. About rhythm, Yeats wrote,

> The purpose of rhythm, it has always seemed to me, is to prolong the moment of contemplation, the moment when we are both asleep and awake, which is the moment of creation, by hushing us with an alluring monotony, while it holds us waiting by variety, to keep us in that state of perhaps real trance, in which the mind liberated from the pressure of the will is unfolded in symbols. (*Essays* 159)

The key to this passage is "alluring monotony." For Yeats, rhythm is neither dead nor flat. Rather, rhythm is "alluring," "hypnotic," "hushing," variable. From it, symbols, as Yeats said, "unfold." If this is so, metaphors may also arise from rhythm. After all, a symbol signifies something, just as a metaphor is comprised of a signifier and a signified. Thus, when rhythm signifies something for us, a mood or a feeling the imagination takes hold of, rhythm may be symbolic and it may be metaphoric.

Yeats, himself, has many poems which use rhythm as metaphor. Consider, as an example, lines taken from "Sailing to Byzantium." At the beginning of the poem, Yeats writes, "That is no country for old men." The younger people and the mating creatures of nature, all the "dying generations," are "Caught in that sensual music" of youthful lust. Because they "commend all summer long / Whatever is begotten, born, and dies," they "neglect / Monuments of unageing intellect." The persona of the poem, implicitly, is such a "monument"; his age and his circumspection may be regarded as evidence of wisdom. Questioning the value of his own life among the younger generation, Yeats sails to the perfection of an imaginary landscape: "And therefore I have sailed the seas and come / To the holy city of Byzantium." Iambic meter notwithstanding (for meter is not necessarily rhythm), the rhythm, here, marches. It is bold and vibrant, a cadence as passionate in its rhythm as the aging man's desire.

Although the poet calls Byzantium "the artifice of eternity," the last section of the poem contains a change in rhythm and in attitude:

> Once out of nature I shall never take
> My bodily form from any natural thing,
> But such a form as Grecian goldsmiths make
> Of hammered gold and gold enamelling
> To keep a drowsy Emperor awake;
> Or set upon a golden bough to sing
> To lords and ladies of Byzantium
> Of what is past, or passing, or to come.

The initial reason for the voyage was to escape neglect; however, if the bird's purpose is to "keep a drowsy Emperor awake," the Emperor's disposition is very similar to the "dying generations."' The poet's songs may be heard, but the message is apt to remain neglected. Metaphorically, the rhythm of the last two lines suggests that very thing: the music is deliberately flat, unlike the march-rhythm in the second stanza. Though the iambic meter may be consistent to lines 15/16, the final rhymed words are reversed in lines 31/32. The word *come* has more of a lulling effect; in the first instance, *come* was an active verb, but in the final position, following as it does a preposition, it is less animate. Furthermore, the caesuras created by the commas between *past* and *or,* and between *passing* and *or,* slow the rhythm from its previous cadence. This slowing creates a deliberate sobering effect. Whenever a poet consciously alters rhythm, as Yeats did, the poet creates metaphorical rhythm: the rhythm is the signifying of the knowledge or emotion the poet wishes to impose upon the poem.

Shklovsky says that poetry is "*attenuated, torturous* speech. Poetic speech is *formed speech* " (61-62). To make language do what we want, we should deliberately twist and conscript the language. We *form* it. As Jakobson reminds us,

> We must recall the two basic modes of arrangement used in verbal behavior, *selection* and *combination*. If 'child' is the topic of the message, the speaker selects one among the extant, more or less similar, nouns like *child, kid, youngster, tot,* all of them equivalent in a certain respect, and then, to comment on this topic, he may select one of the semantically cognate verbs—*sleeps, dozes, nods, naps*. Both chosen words combine in the speech chain. The selection is produced on the basis of equivalence, similarity and dissimilarity, synonymy and antonymy, while the combination, the build-up of the sequence, is based on contiguity. (3: 27)

Selection and combination is not random. It *is not* an opening of flood gates, as I noted previously, to let the poem fill with words; it *is* the poet's carefully devised, imagined, plotted manipulation of language.

A good example of this in Yeats's poetry is found in "A Coat":

> I made my song a coat
> Covered with embroideries
> Out of old mythologies
> From heel to throat;
> But the fools caught it,
> Wore it in the world's eyes
> As though they'd wrought it.
> Song, let them take it,
> For there's more enterprise
> In walking naked.

The first line is an example of deliberate word-combining. *Song* and *coat* are so dissimilar, the combination makes excellent estrangement; in fact, the combination dominates the poem's whole direction. Also, the combining creates ambiguity. How are we to read the first line? Perhaps the poet provided a coat for his song, and clothed it in "embroideries" of "old mythologies." If this is the case, the adornment is surface texture only—it has nothing to do with the song's significance. Or, we can read a metaphor of extreme contrast into the line. Implicitly, the poet makes his song *into* a coat. In the first example, the song wears the embroidered coat; in the second, the song is the embroidered coat. Either reading is pleasing, but the second is more complex and delighting.

The song, or poem, is every bit and particle fabric and embroidery. The poetry, though a new creation, is an old mythology. If the first reading is preferred, the poet addresses his song and tells it to let the fools have the adorned coat; thus, the song will walk naked. However, if we prefer the second reading, the *it* of the eighth line refers back to *song* in emphatic designation, and not to *coat* (for the song *is* the coat). Thus, the fools can have the adorned song. This leaves the poet "walking naked." He has no song; he must work with the materials of his own nakedness.[3]

As combinations such as these are made, so, too, are combinations in "sound texture" (Jakobson 2: 356). Jakobson says, "In poetry, any conspicuous similarity in sound is evaluated in respect to similarity and/or dissimilarity in meaning. But Pope's alliterative precept to poets—'the sound must seem an Echo of the sense'—has a wider application" (3: 44). Word combinations commit the poet to select according to appropriate sound textures.

To understand this concept better, let us take a look at the first stanza of Yeats's "Two Songs of a Fool":

> A speckled cat and a tame hare
> Eat at my hearthstone
> And sleep there;
> And both look up to me alone
> For learning and defence
> As I look up to Providence.

Sound texture is involved in the disbursement of mono- and double-syllabic words. The tonal aspect of syllables in these words is metaphorical. The adjectives *speckled* and *tame* modify *cat* and *hare*. The concrete quality of the double syllabic word and the shortness of the monosyllabic one create a subtle commonness. The sound is low, calm—tame, like the hare. Metaphorically, the low sound is equivalent to the lowest link of the poem's Chain of Being. The verbs appointed to the animals follow the same pattern. All three—*eat, sleep,* and *look*—are monosyllablics. The next link in the chain belongs to the higher order of humankind. The animals "look up" to the fool. However, since he is of a higher order, the words belong to a higher order of diction. They sound loftier, and they are more abstract and affected than those words that modified the animals. The majority of words appointed to the man are double-syllabics: *hearthstone, alone, learning, defence.* Of these, only *hearthstone* is concrete and the rest are abstract. The abstract quality makes a metaphorical point about the state of humanity. The man resides in the concrete, animal world, but he falls victim to the ambiguities of *learning* and *defence.* He is *alone,* and the ambiguity of that word suggests either "me all alone" or "only me." *Alone* is the first word that elevates the diction level from the tangible to the intangible. The animal's deference to man is equivalent to the man's looking up to God in Providence. *Providence* occupies the highest level of abstraction, and the Latinate word possesses a sound metaphorically consistent to the highest, ethereal link in the chain.[4]

Jakobson poses an additional interesting question: "Is there a semantic propinquity, a sort of simile between rhyming lexical units, as in dove-love, light-bright, place-space, name-fame?" (3: 38). This, I think, could make a marvelous defamiliarization and an interesting study of metaphor. For example (and not a great or an original one), consider this off rhyme: "The Devil is Evil." This "rhyming lexical unit" at least illustrates on an elementary level the thing Jakobson is talking about. The Devil is evil; simultaneously, he is all Evil. A better example might be the "semantic propinquity" between *romance* and *chance*. Pursuit of romance requires chance; furthermore, chance and romance may be perceived as forms of gambling. To take this to an extreme, someone certain of failure in love may understand the equivalences between *romance* and *no chance*.

I would guess that in the body of a great poet's work, we would find a number of "semantic propinquities" making metaphors. I turn to Yeats's poems again. Many of his poems address his unrequited love of Maud Gonne. If he had written somewhere in his work, "My love is gone," he would have implied a "semantic propinquity" with a poor pun extending into metaphor: "My love is gone"; "My love is Gonne"; "Gone is Gonne." Fortunately, Yeats does not succumb to such easiness. However, in an early version of "The Lamentation of the Old Pensioner," written three years after he had met Maud Gonne (Ellmann and O'Clair 110, 116-17), Yeats writes in the final two lines of the poem: "The well-known faces are all gone / And the fret lies on me." At the height of his infatuation with Maud Gonne, every face is her face; simultaneously, because she had already refused his love, all those Gonne faces are absent. If Jakobson's point is valid, this is a better example.[5]

Similarly, many of Yeats's poems symbolize swans as perfected love. "The Wild Swans at Coole" and "Among School Children," in particular, are examples which find Yeats dwelling upon the loss of perfect love. In these poems, *swan* is implicitly juxtaposed to *Gonne*; the tension occurs when the symbol of perfect love is placed in opposition with the memory of imperfect love. Note the near rhyme: swan-Gonne. Yeats's readers might understand, after a time, when he speaks of swans he is often indirectly speaking about Maud Gonne.

Prosody and meter may help the poet to make metaphors, too. When the poet alters the meter of a line, he draws attention to the substitution. When the reader's attention is diverted to that moment of substitution, it is a perfect location for metaphor. In Yeats's "A Song from 'The Player Queen,'" one will find the poet making metrical substitutions several times. These substitutions create metrical metaphor because they suggest in the motion of the line what the line itself says. Examine, for the sake of illustration, the third quatrain. A scansion of the lines reveals this pattern:

˘ ´ ˘ ´ ˘ ´ ˘ ´
She pulled | the thread | and bit | the thread
˘ ´ ˘ ´ ˘ ´
And made | a gold | en gown,
˘ ´ ˘ ´ ˘ ˘ ´ ˘ ´
And wept | because | she had dreamt | that I
˘ ´ ˘ ´ ˘ ´
Was born | to wear | a crown.

The poem is a series of five ballad stanzas in common measure. In other words, the first and third lines of each quatrain are straight iambic tetrameter; the second and fourth lines are iambic trimeter. However, Yeats substitutes in every third line. The stanza above contains the anapestic "she had dreamt." While some prosodists might argue that this foot contains an elision (of "she had" to read "she'd") and that it is actually iambic, Yeats has not provided any clear evidence, as he does in some poems through punctuation or syncope, that such elision is intended. Thus, the allowable anapestic scansion reveals several things. First, its accent falls heavily upon *dreamt.* The many consonants surrounding the short vowel sound require a more deliberate reading; the anapest slows the line and provides a pause to enable the difficult articulation. Secondly, this anapestic substitution metaphorically affects the mood of the line. The deliberate slowness equals the seriousness delegated to the accented word. The movement of the poem is suspended, just as the dream suspends reality.[6]

Besides prosody, grammatical structure avails itself to metaphor. Gerard Manley Hopkins said that "the structure of poetry is that of continuous parallelism" (84). This parallelism, Jakobson says, "is a referral from one sign to a similar one . . . , present or implied in the same context . . ." (*Framework* 22-23). Grammatical structure as metaphor, however, is a relatively new study. As Jakobson says,

> No open-minded student of poetry would deny the legitimacy and significance of monographic studies devoted to questions of metrics or strophics, alliterations or rhymes, or to questions of poets' vocabulary, whereas the varied problems of poets' grammatical means have remained for the most part nearly unnoticed. (3: 767)

Accordingly, we should consider what grammatical disbursement does for metaphor.[7] Yeats's poetry provides us with numerous examples of "grammatical equivalences." We can look at a fairly short piece and still find a wealth of these complexities. Consider, then, "There":

> There all the barrel-hoops are knit,
> There all the serpent-tails are bit,
> There all the gyres converge in one,
> There all the planets drop in the Sun.

Doing what Jakobson suggests, we can chart the following combinations:

	Adverb	**Adjective**	**Noun**	**Verb** (present plural indicative of *be* + past participle)
Line 1:	There	all	barrel-hoops	are knit
Line 2:	There	all	serpent-tails	are bit

The pattern is identical in the first two lines. No grammatical variations occur. However, Yeats changes the grammatical sequence in the third and fourth lines:

	Adverb	**Adjective**	**Noun**	**Verb**	**Prep**	**Adj. Noun-Substitution**
Line 3:	There	all	gyres	converge	in	one (*gyre*, implicitly)
						Noun
Line 4:	There	all	planets	drop	in	Sun

Yeats retains the initial "adverb + adjective" sequence in all four lines, creating anaphora. Anaphora's grammatical structure, in this example, produces metaphor. Repetition of *there* forces us to focus upon an unseen, ethereal location, a place obviously not *here. There* belongs to the "other world" Yeats so often looks for in his verse. The repetition of *all* reinforces the convergence we find in this poem. When *all* is repeated the fourth time, the word becomes weighted heavily in its final position. In this manner, the poet has created a funnel effect—everything draws downward to a point. This opposes the pattern the noun sequence establishes. In line one, the noun is concrete; however, the nouns become increasingly abstract in subsequent lines. Line two is concrete, but more ambiguous than line one. In line three, *gyres* is airy and intangible, though belonging to the earth; and, line four's *planets* exist outside the tangible world. Hence, *planets* is the most distant noun. Though the anaphora draws things downward, the allotment of concrete nouns to abstract ones sets the funnel on its wide base and points the concrete or narrowed end upward. The grammar creates what Yeats's gyres did; it becomes Yeats's concentric cones.

The primary grammatical alteration occurs in the verb sequences. The real verbs of lines three and four are more aggressive than the copula/participle combinations of one and two. These verbs thrust the poem into the Sun's consuming gravity. Furthermore, in the first two lines the verbs tie linear images into hoops. The metal bands that become barrel-hoops have their ends welded together by the *are knit* verb, and the serpents bite their own tails to form a hoop. The verbs in lines three and four gather up all hoops, including those of gyres and orbiting planets, and merge them into the fiery hoop of the Sun. Thus, if the poem is *about* the convergence of all spirals, the grammatical system also spirals.[8]

Jakobson also discusses the "grammar of traffic signals." That grammar utilizes "a signal code, where a yellow light when combined with a green warns that free passage is close to being stopped and when combined with red announces the approaching cessation of the stoppage; such a yellow signal offers a close analogue to the verbal completive aspect" (3: 35). This idea strikes my curiosity. I find Yeats using numerous signal codes, and these suggest parallel metaphors. Certain grammatical constituents, nouns and verbs especially, suggest "warnings" when combined with other, similar units. In poetry, the "warning" is a declaration that commands attention. Take, for example, Yeats's many references to swans. When Yeats places swans in natural settings, the warning indicates the sensation of melancholy. When swans are juxtaposed to mythological elements, we find violence. When this violence occurs it results from unnatural lust or desire. When melancholy occurs, we find failure of the man in his own decrepitude or in his pursuit of love. The metaphors—swan/nature = melancholy; swan/myth = violence; melancholy = age/unrequited love; violence = lust—generate from the grammatical presences in the poetry.[9]

A poem's form may also suggest metaphor. The relationship of section to section, stanza to stanza, not only creates tension, it embeds metaphor in that tension. The structure of Yeats's "Leda and the Swan" is a good illustration. Notice the violence of the first quatrain and the terror in the second:

> A sudden blow: the great wings beating still
> Above the staggering girl, her thighs caressed
> By the dark webs, her nape caught in his bill,
> He holds her helpless breast upon his breast.
>
> How can those terrified vague fingers push
> The feathered glory from her loosening thighs?
> And how can body, laid in that white rush,
> But feel the strange heart beating where it lies?

Metaphorically, these two stanzas equal the violence and terror found in the sestet:

> A shudder in the loins engenders there
> The broken wall, the burning roof and tower
> And Agamemnon dead.
>   Being so caught up,
> So mastered by the brute blood of the air,
> Did she put on his knowledge with his power
> Before the indifferent beak could let her drop?

The octave is the private or microcosmic occurrence; however, this *is* also the pattern of the sestet's universal or macrocosmic occurences. The god's rape of a mortal is as unnatural and as violent as the events that shape history: Clytemnestra's murder of Agamemnon, committed with the aid of her adulterous lover; and, Troy's destruction resultant from Paris's lust for and kidnapping of Helen. Leda's terror and vagueness are equal to the terror and vagueness of power and knowledge. Other structural metaphors occur, too. The broken line in the sestet is a metaphor of the broken wall; the broken wall is a metaphor for the broken hymen. These particular metaphors—joined in the poem by rhythm, rhyme, assonance, consonance, symbol, and whatever else Yeats can *make* work in the poem—make "Leda and the Swan" one of the most successful poems ever written. It is virtually flawless.

The points and examples discussed in this chapter are intended to resolve some important poetic issues, as well as show their function in Yeats's work. These various metaphorical techniques can, in part, give poems depth. The more multifaceted a poem is, the more likely the poem might be a lasting one. The poem is very similar to what Georges Poulet says about art: "Statues make me want to circle around them, vases make me want to turn them in my hands. I wonder why. Isn't it because they give me the illusion that there is something in them which, from a different angle, I might be able to see?" (351). Because the poem is a work of art, it must allow its audience to circle around it, to see it from different perspectives. Although metaphor appears at times to be a means by which poets can make their poetry exotic, this is not its function. Ricoeur says, "The work of resemblance has to be appropriate and homogeneous to the deviance and the oddness and the freshness of the semantic innovation itself" (145). The innovations I have discussed are "not those that interrupt reading and distort or divert it" (148). Rather, they enhance and supplement those readings, correcting an interpretive emptiness. Wayne C. Booth says that metaphor is "a quest for ways to improve culture and myself"; it is "a search for a cure" (62). Similarly, a study of metaphor and its assignment to poetry is a way to improve our understanding not only of literature but of ourselves. For, if poetic craftsmanship declines, there may be a parallel decline in society's interest in language. Both are products of the same degenerative disease. A poet such as Yeats knows that the work must not dictate itself to the writer. The poet works to cheat chance, for as Barthes says, "The work of art is what man wrests from chance" (305). Secondly, as poets learn to control their writing, they discover what Yeats meant by "indefinable . . . , disembodied powers" (*Essays* 157). As Baudelaire said, "There exists in the word, in the verb, something sacred which prohibits us from viewing [writing] as a mere game of chance. To manipulate language with wisdom is to practice . . . evocative sorcery" (qtd. in Jakobson 3: 769). We learn, in a "variability of meanings, . . . a continuously inventive sweep" (Jakobson 2: 659).

In the following chapters, I shall examine Yeats's use of the kinds of metaphors discussed above in conjunction with broader verbal structures—or concepts. The metaphors of rhyme, rhythm, grammar, sound, and form often work through the apparatus of the conceptual metaphor. Specifically, the concept is a complex thought comprised of a set of disparate or estranged notions linked into a metaphorical sequence of equivalence. Unlike the theme, which is generally a statement of one attitude (as in, "The theme of the poem is humankind's inhumanity to humankind."), the concept is a sequence of attitudes or ideas linked metaphorically to another sequence of attitudes or ideas. The concept states, implicitly, that notions *X, Y,* and *Z* are equivalent to a second set of notions: *X*1, *Y*1, and *Z*1. Thus, rather than make a fairly simple thematic interpretation of an author's work, the study of conceptual metaphors is much more rewarding. As I will discuss in Chapter 2, some critics have said that Yeats's theme is escape. The conceptual metaphor considers the notions that comprise the concept of *escape:* dissatisfaction, desire of ease, paradise. These are linked metaphorically to notions comprising the second concept, *embrace* (or *acceptance*): added burden, failure to attain paradise, heroism. The notions of the first concept are juxtaposed to the notions of the second; though disparate, the metaphorical sequence makes them equal. That is, *escape* is *embrace.* The conceptual complex undergoes a metaphorical transmutation when tested under a variety of circumstances or when applied to numerous illustrations. Regardless of illustrative variability, the concept remains consistently patterned. Thus, the conceptual metaphor says first that Complex 1 = Complex 2; second, it says Complex 1/Complex 2 = the validation. In Yeats's case, the validation is his body of poems.

The conceptual metaphor moves well beyond thematic issues into those that concern the construction of belief-systems and the dismantling of others. It exemplifies the redesigning of the poet's internal and external universes. If God has spoken the Word which became the world, the poet no less speaks one's own complexities into existence.[10] The conceptual metaphor is "the terrible novelty of light" ("High Talk"); it is "riddled with light" ("The Cold Heaven"). Thus, it is revelation, epiphany, the poetic exposure of soul and intellect, and the creation and solution of aesthetic puzzling.

Though other conceptual metaphors exist in Yeats's work, those discussed in the following chapters are most prevalent. In Chapter 2, I will analyze the early conceptual metaphors of the island wanderer. These include concepts about island paradises, about the hero's responsibilities, about beauty, and about escape and embrace. In Chapter 3, the anima bruta metaphor illustrates Yeats's concepts of beast and blood, and of violent and sensual passion. In Chapters 4 and 5, metaphors of art and architecture pertain to aesthetic and psychological concepts, as well as to complexes pertaining to human decrepitude and to eternity. The metaphor of dissolution, under discussion in Chapter 6, examines concepts of poetic structure as well as the dissolution of belief systems and of the human body.

CHAPTER 2

WANDERING AENGUS: YEATS'S EARLY METAPHORICAL PATTERNS

Yeats's early poems, specifically those found in *Crossways* and *The Rose*, as well as a smaller number from *In the Seven Woods*, pose problems for critical discourse. They seem unfocused thematically and inconsistent when compared to the deliberateness of poems from Yeats's middle and later periods. The mature mind of the poet had not yet developed the cohesive, elaborate system upon which Yeats would build many of his later poems. Thus, these poems seem estranged from each other, grasping at pre-Raphaelite and Romantic themes as they court Irish nationalism. The poems seem belonging to an age long past, not just to the milieu of the first and second generations of Romantics and those Irish poets he read, but also to the 18th Century and those poets whose work was founded upon pastoral and national subjects.[1] A few of the early poems, however, are quite remarkable and memorable.

The early poems allow us to trace the development of a poet whose greatness is evident in the early work. Rather than evaluate the early poems against the later ones, I intend to isolate the early poems as much as possible in order to give them a sound metaphorical reading. Many of the metaphorical experiments Yeats makes lay the foundation upon which he frames his most successful later pieces. I agree with David Daiches who writes:

> I do not want to make too great a claim for the quality and interest of Yeats's earlier poetry; but I believe that a fair amount of it is of real interest, not simply to the pedant interested in charting a map of development or a researcher trying to classify themes and techniques, but to the reader and critic concerned with the kinds of imagination

and the uses of language out of which poetry develops . . . . (48-49)

This approximates my specific interest in the early poems. Yeats's young poetic imagination gives rise to the "great-rooted blossomer" ("Among School Children") of the mature imagination. In the early poems begin the roots to Yeats's symbol, language, invention, and metaphor.

The early poems seem to wander from one subject or theme to the next. This accounts for that apparent variability mentioned previously. Consequently, the tendency of the criticism upon the early poems is diversity and contradiction. However, an aesthetic principle links the variable poems together; this principle is metaphor. If we do a metaphorical reading of the early poems, we can avoid the classifications belonging to other critics. We can avoid the formulation of safe and nearly accurate statements, and we do not risk the obvious, as Alex Zwerdling does, by saying the early poems deal with the "exotic material of . . . *Mosada*, 'Anashaya and Vijaya,' or 'The Indian Upon God,'" and how "these are later 'eliminated and replaced by a concentration on strictly Irish subjects in the years between 1888 . . . and 1899'" (36). Such discussions exclude the fact that the early poems also deal with shepherds and with heroes who desire something other than what the temporal world offers. They deal with imagined country and island landscapes. Metaphor clarifies and reconciles the relationship of these exotic, Irish, shepherd, hero, field and island subjects.

The first of Yeats's conceptual metaphors has to do with his notions of the artist and the hero. Generally, the aesthetic man is a wandering hero, someone apart from the "common herd." An outsider, an exotic, he is a visionary, able to live simultaneously in the physical realm and in imaginary worlds. For example, in "The Song of the Happy Shepherd," the first poem from *Crossways,* the poet asserts what will be his life-long belief that art is the ultimate and desirable alternative to reality.[2] The poet writes:

The woods of Arcady are dead,
And over is their antique joy;
Of old the world on dreaming fed;
Grey Truth is now her painted toy;
Yet still she turns her restless head:
But O, sick children of the world,
Of all the many changing things
In dreary dancing past us whirled,
To the cracked tune that Chronos sings,
Words alone are certain good.

The opening lines of this poem pose immediate problems. While the poem concentrates upon a pastoral setting, it is not typically pastoral for "The woods of Arcady are dead, / And over is their antique joy." If the woods are dead, as is the joy the woods provided the pastoral shepherds, we must question how this can be the song of a happy shepherd. All that happiness seems lost; the world, which once fed upon dreams, now must play with "Grey Truth." Note the contradiction found in the metaphor "Grey Truth is now her painted toy." Truth as toy is a simple enough metaphor: the world pursues reality via philosophy. Yet Truth is grey, not black nor white—it possesses no contrast, it is all equally pale, ambiguous, hazy. This, juxtaposed to the word *painted*, creates an interesting estrangement since the word connotes something bright and colorful because of the context of "toy."

By and large, the contradictory metaphor forms the foundation for those poems which comprise Yeats's most memorable work. If truth is a grey-painted toy, it is one that does not satisfy the world, let alone the poet's imagination or soul. The world "turns her restless head"; her "sick children" are warned that time (Chronos) sings a "cracked tune" and that there are "many changing things" "dancing past us." This establishes a pattern that will become especially important to Yeats later on, what I call "the metaphor of dissolution" in Chapter 6. Things pass away, dissolve, die. Although Yeats will make exceptional use of this metaphor later, for now he must comfort himself, as the world must, upon the one remaining virtue: "Words alone are certain good."

In this line, too, is another key metaphor. Words equal "certain good." Nothing else, explicitly, is good but words. Yeats considers the ramifications of such a notion in the following lines:

> Where are now the warring kings,
> Word be-mockers? By the Rood
> Where are now the warring kings?
> An idle word is now their glory,
> By the stammering schoolboy said,
> Reading some entangled story:
> The kings of the old time are dead;
> The wandering earth herself may be
> Only a sudden flaming word,
> In clanging space a moment heard,
> Troubling the endless reverie.

The "warring kings" of heroic antiquity, the "word be-mockers," are dead. Thus, we cannot find goodness in them. Additionally, the kings despise words if they would mock them. Ironically, word-mockers live only in words stammered by schoolboys. What the "stammering schoolboy" knows—as Yeats himself knows—and what we should know, is that even stammered words and the "entangled story" are good because they are words. An "*idle* word" (emphasis added) may also be, as pun allows, an *idol* word, one to be revered or worshipped. "The wandering earth herself may be / Only a sudden flaming word"; if earth is, it, too, is good. Thus, before Derrida ever wrote about how there is no non-metaphoric language and how everything that exists exists because of language's usurpation and signification, Yeats makes much the same deconstructive claim.[3] Deconstructionists would never say we may trust words, but Yeats's concept of the originary value of language is at least consistent.

Notice, too, the metrical metaphor of "In clanging space a moment heard, / Troubling the endless reverie." A scansion of the lines reveals the following accentual patterns:

˘ ´ ˘ ´ ˘ ´ ˘ ´

In clang | ing space | a mo | ment heard,

´ ˘ ˘ ´ ˘ ´ ˘ ´

Troubling | the end | less rev | erie.

The first line is iambic tetrameter; however, the second line's trochaic first foot ("Troubling") upsets the iambic pattern. Metaphorically, the line is the "clanging space" of a moment. Of essential note, too, is the function of the final word *reverie.* The "reverie" is supposed to be "endless"; thus, the word reaches out into the white-space at the line's end.

But humankind seeks beyond language's pure function, corrupting the use of signification, misusing it. The "word be-mockers" are "warring kings"; from such people not only "Grey Truth" comes but all other worldly corruptions. The world is restless because corrupt humanity will not let her sleep peacefully; her children are sick because they have fallen victim to the corruption. Yeats's persona, the shepherd, warns us about such things by telling us not to "worship dusty deeds," not to "hunger fiercely after truth" because all it will do is breed more corruption in "new dreams, new dreams." Instead, he says to find truth "in thine own heart." He says not to heed any word of those "who follow with the optic glass / The whirling ways of the stars," for "dead is all their human truth." Instead, the shepherd says we should

Go gather by the humming sea
Some twisted, echo-harbouring shell,
And to its lips thy story tell,
And they thy comforters will be,
Rewarding in melodious guile

> Thy fretful words a little while,
> Till they shall singing fade in ruth
> And die a pearly brotherhood; . . .

"Sing," the shepherd commands, but with these restrictions: the shepherd makes the shell the ear for whatever words we have to pass on; it is an "echo-harbouring shell," where our words will lie in deposit until they fade. The words are not left where others might devise "Grey Truths" from them.

Here, then, is both the irony of poetry and of the metaphor of the aesthetic individual as the wandering hero. If "words alone are certain good," and if we are to sing our fading stories to the lips of an "echo-harbouring shell," is the poet not doing exactly what the shepherd warns against? Does the poet not leave words behind out of which others will form "grey truth"? Perhaps, but the corruption is not the poet's, for the poet starts with a primary pursuit, singing into the poem as the shepherd would the echo-harbouring shell. The shepherd could sing to us, too, through the shell, if we allowed ourselves that "pearly brotherhood."

The last stanza completes certain of these metaphorical notions:

> I must be gone: there is a grave
> Where daffodil and lily wave,
> And I would please the hapless faun,
> Buried under the sleepy ground,
> With mirthful songs before the dawn.
> His shouting days with mirth were crowned;
> And still I dream he treads the lawn,
> Walking ghostly in the dew,
> Pierced by my glad singing through,
> My songs of old earth's dreamy youth:
> But ah! she dreams not now; dream thou!
> For fair are poppies on the brow:
> Dream, dream, for this is also sooth.

Yeats diverts our attention from those who misuse words and create for the world what he called "manifold illusion" ("Meru"), and draws our attention to the faun that lies "buried under the sleepy ground." Doing so, Yeats creates a Romantic transference to an alternative reality, much as we find in Coleridge's "This Lime Tree Bower My Prison." The Shepherd remarks that he still dreams the faun "treads the lawn, / Walking ghostly in the dew." However, this shocks him into reality, and reality is not where he wants to be—its corruption of truth and of body is unpleasant. The faun is dead; like it, the world "dreams not now," because the world is dead in its false pursuit of "Grey Truth." Those of us who remain alive, however, are invited to dream and to enjoy the opiate sensation of those dreams ("fair are poppies on the brow"). Like words, dreams are creations of the imagination. Thus, the happy shepherd says, "Dream, dream, for this is also sooth."

Compare this poem, briefly, to its companion piece, "The Sad Shepherd." As Richard Peterson notes, the shepherd of the first poem "is happy because he believes that 'Words alone are certain good' and that no truth exists 'Saving in thine own heart'" (55). The second shepherd is unhappy, however, because he "was a man whom Sorrow named his friend, / And he, of his high comrade Sorrow dreaming, / Went walking with slow steps . . . ." The Sad Shepherd fails to pursue what the Happy Shepherd suggests is the way to happiness: to trust in words and the heart's truth, to sing, and to dream. Sorrow, the metaphorical parallel of "Grey Truth," is the culprit. Rather than search the recesses of his own heart, the Sad Shepherd dreams about Sorrow, losing himself to his own self pity. He has a story to sing, but it is not a pure story. That is, it is not a song of the heart or of the imagination. It is muddled with Sorrrow's influence. When the shepherd "called loudly to the stars to bend / From their pale thrones and comfort him," he has become one of those "starry men" noted in the previous poem. When he attempts, as the Happy Shepherd directs, to "gather by the humming sea, / Some twisted, echo-harboring shell," and sing his story to it, he expects that his words,

> re-echoing, shall send
> Their sadness through a hollow, pearly heart;
> And my own tale again for me shall sing,
> And my own whispering words be comforting,
> And lo! my ancient burden may depart.

However, the shell "changed all he sang to inarticulate moan" and forgot him. What he sings to the shell were not "words alone," but words derived from Sorrow's influence. He sings sorrow to the shell; it consumes the sound, but the self-pitying song turns into a moan. Since the original articulation is not pure, it can only transform into gutteral noise once it occupies the recesses of the shell. Look closely at the dissonance of this particular line. Assonance and its attendant euphony occur only once, in *changed* and *sang*. Otherwise, the vowel and consonant sounds metaphorically suggest noise, peaked especially in the sound of the polysyllabic *inarticulate* while all other words are monosyllabics.

The juxtapositioning of these two poems poses a very Blakean structure.[4] Antithesis creates conflict, yet from this opposition we might derive some harmony, some reconcilement of life's extremities. The conflicts—sad shepherd opposed to happy shepherd, words of "certain good" opposed to words of another kind—shape for us indispensable metaphorical relationships. What we find in the late poems begins here. The conflicts Yeats wages between the happy and the sad shepherd, and the significance of words, become the battlegrounds for the poet throughout his life. Furthermore, here Yeats constructs the foundation of a metaphorical system that will support his warring. Though it seems occasionally to lead him astray, the system always draws Yeats back to the alternative reality that art alone provides.

Consider, too, some of the equivalences Yeats established here. A listing of metaphorical relationships (*A* is *A*1) will reveal several:

A	*A*1
woods or Arcady	something dead, the past; regrets over loss.
the dead; past; regrets	loss of joy.
loss of joy	usurpment by Grey Truth.
Grey Truth	restlessness, sick children, change, dreary dancing, time without syncopation (a cracked tune), dusty deeds, starry men, hearts rent in twain.

The pattern descends to the tremendous weighting of the negative *A*1 component. The greater the frequency of the equivalences, the heavier load the metaphor carries. As mathematical equations function, the metaphor functions. The loss of Arcady is equal to all the trouble found in the last *A*1 listing.

To complete his poem, Yeats works out his antithetical balances. If one form of good is lost, some other good must replace it. In this case, good *is* words:

A	*A*1
Words	good
idle word	glory of kings
flaming word	wandering earth
words	(implicitly) the truth in thine own heart
words	comfort (as spoken into the shell)
words	singing
singing	dreaming

The linking pattern seen in the first listing occurs here with some variance. All components of *A* are *words*, and these are equivalent to all members of the *A*1 column. Consequently, all members of *A*1 are equivalent to each other. Furthermore, the earth is used metaphorically, too: the earth is mother. Curiously, when the mother is sick and cannot dream (and, implicitly, cannot sing), the children of the earth must dream. If *we* speak our dreams (for we are the earth's children), we must speak them to a shell. The shell, with its womb-like, echo-harbouring shape, is a mother metaphor. The earth wanders; similarly, the shell's twistings force the song to wander through its passages. We are told in the closing lines of "The Sad Shepherd" the earth once dreamed, but since it does not dream now, we must dream, we must sing, we must use words to speak the truth of ourselves. Yeats suggests in these poems how the individual might be guided through the universe happily. The persona is not *just* a shepherd of animals, but a shepherd of *all* humanity. He does not sing philosophy or grey truths but the truths of the heart. His life is a song inside the shell of the universe; just as his song lives and fades, so does ours. Words make us significant. They shape and define our existence, bringing us out of the haze sorrow makes of life. The stars that "laugh on and sing alway," the dewdrops that are "always listening, / . . . for the sound of their own dropping," are doing what the Sad Shepherd ought to be doing—listening to the music of self, not sorrow's tune.

These points comprise Yeats's first metaphorical pattern: in the one poem, we find a blessed life, not in the hills of Arcady, but in words, songs, dreams, all of them configurations of the imagination. In the second, we find a cursed life, not in the hills of Arcady, but not in words, songs, dreams, either; the curse comes from something external encroaching upon the internal. Happiness is found in the pure, internalized experience of the imagination. Outside forces wage violence against the self and soul. Yeats would battle these oppositions throughout his life and poetry. External stimuli always burdened Yeats, yet he simultaneously perfected his art in defiance against that stimuli. Thus, even Yeats's early poems illustrated the importance of the artistic pursuit. Only there could perfection of soul and art exist, reconciled to each other. The alternative would have been to be lost in and forgotten by the real world. The metaphor of the wandering hero, then, is Yeats's illustration of how the aesthetic individual pursues the artifact originating in the heart.

This metaphor is illustrated again in the Indian poems, specifically "The Indian Upon God" and "The Indian to his Love." However, in these poems Yeats links the first metaphorical concept to a second. Paradise is an island in the imagination. Not the longed for mythic worlds of Eden or Heaven, Paradise is constructed in the mind and heart. As Thomas Byrd says, "The Indian poems are meditations on the bittersweet mood found in settings that symbolize tranquillity and static being. The peace of the setting cannot be fully realized by those who inhabit it, whether they be human or animal" (84). Specifically, the Indian protagonist and the other characters in these poems live in what seems paradise; however, they seek to express paradise in external terms rather than in heart-felt truth. As Harbans Bachchan notes, "In 'The Indian Upon God' the idea conveyed is that everybody conceives of God in his own image. The moorfowl thinks that God is an 'undying moorfowl,' the lotus, that He is a huge lotus with 'His petals wide,' the roebuck, that 'He is a gentle roebuck' and the peacock, that 'He is a monstrous peacock'" (47). This is an inversion of the traditional creation myth: the creatures create God in their image. Those who give God signification, attributing incorrectly their existence to their creator, cannot appreciate the paradise they are born into. The Indian, significantly, does not shape God; perhaps this is so because his "spirit rocked in sleep and sighs." Though he is not restricted by self-imposed belief systems, he is little better off than the creatures. He wanders, implicitly dissatisfied with the philosophies of the other creatures, yet searching for something of his own. "The Indian to his Love" follows much the same discourse. Here, Yeats creates what seems an island paradise, though something remains unsettled at the poem's conclusion. "The island dreams under the dawn / And great boughs drop tranquillity"; however, despite the dance of peahens on a "smooth lawn," "a parrot sways upon a tree, / Raging at his own image in the enamelled sea." The mirror image here is not unlike the mirror images of God and creation noted in the previous poem. The parrot rages at its reflection, no less than we are apt to rage against God. In this paradise, the island is part of the world, microcosm in macrocosm. If the parrot rages as we do, then the peahens must dance their lives away as we must. The lovers disembark a "lonely ship." Metaphorically, they leave the larger world for the smaller. However, if the parallel structure holds consistent, the island is a "lonely ship," too. Take note of the contradiction: lovers are lonely, even when they are together.

Note, too, the next mirror image; the lovers will

> wander ever with woven hands,
> Murmuring softly lip to lip,
> Along the grass, along the sands,
> Murmuring how far away are the unquiet lands:
> How we alone of mortals are . . . .

The lovers murmuring "lip to lip" is the mirror image. The lovers reflect one another. However, this paradise is not exactly an unquiet land. The dreaming island is imperfect. First, let us scan these three lines:

´ ˘ ˘ ´ ˘ ´ ˘ ´

Murmur | ing soft | ly lip | to lip,

˘ ´ ˘ ´ ˘ ´ ˘ ´

Along | the grass, | along | the sands,

´ ˘ ˘ ˘ ´ ˘ ´ ˘ ˘ ˘ ´ ˘ ´

Murmuring | how far | away | are the | unqui | et lands:

A considerable amount of sound attends these lines, and, metaphorically, the island. Though the lines are largely iambic, substitution occurs, creating the same tonal effect noted in "The Sad Shepherd." The first line contains a trochee ("Murmur") in the first foot; the third line contains a dactyl ("Murmuring") in the first foot and a pyrrhic ("are the") in the fourth foot. Granted, some prosodists might read the fourth foot as iambic. The word *are*, however, does not merit a full accent (thus, my pyrrhic scansion). Notice, too, how Yeats has changed from tetrameter lines to a hexameter line, or an Alexandrine. While the Alexandrine is not unusual for pentameter stanzas, it does seem somewhat unusual for tetrameter. The metrical metaphor suggests the noise of both the island paradise and the "unquiet lands." Certainly, though, the lovers are not "far away" from "unquiet lands." Second, consider the connotations of the words Yeats chose to use here. *Alone* is ambiguous; it suggests *loneliness*, or it suggests *away from*. If the first definition is correct, we trust love will keep them happy, grow "an Indian star, / A meteor of the burning heart." But loneliness casts them into a paradise without God. Adam and Eve hid from God when they sinned, but this couple hides unnecessarily—where God does not dwell there is no retribution. Something is wrong, and the last stanza changes its tone radically to indicate that troubled spirit. The "quiet boughs" become "heavy boughs"; the dancing peahens and raging parrot, much stronger emblems than the poem's last bird, are replaced by a dove "that moans and sighs a hundred days." When the lovers die, they will not rest. Their "shades will rove" in eternal somnabulism, with "vapoury footsole by the water's drowsy blaze." Byrd states, "A tension is . . . created between the static peace and restless wandering, indicating an unconscious awareness that the temple and the island, or the state of knowing all forms of life, is not the end of the search. The seeker, possessed by a spirit of restlessness, must still meditate and wander until he reaches the true goal" (84). This "true goal" is the one the Happy Shepherd has found in words and in the heart's truth. It is the goal Yeats will pursue for years.

Notice, too, the similarities between the Indian and the Shepherd. Both live isolated or removed from the rest of the world. Locating these characters in such a manner is metaphorically the placement of the artist, virtually outside, looking upon the world. In Yeats's case, the artist looks in upon a self-created world. Not surprisingly, we find the metaphor of the isolated artist coupled to isolated landscape. If the "hills of Arcady are dead," there must be an alternative location in which the artistic imagination can reside. In "The Song of the Happy Shepherd" and in "The Sad Shepherd," the characters are deposited upon the beach (where else could they find "echo-harbouring" shells?), and not in their pastoral fields. "The Indian upon God" and "The Indian to his Love" are similarly isolated. The former poem finds its protagonist "along the water's edge," too; however, a significant shift of place occurs in the latter poem. Now, Yeats tells us specifically the place is an island, set "far away" from "the unquiet lands." Thus, in these four poems alone, we find a pattern shaping a metaphor for art, where the isolated artist withdraws willfully from the real world.

Compare these poems to "The Lake Isle of Innisfree":

> I will arise and go now, and go to Innisfree,
> And a small cabin build there, of clay and wattles made:
> Nine bean-rows will I have there, a hive for the honey-bee,
> And live alone in the bee-loud glade.

Here, Yeats illustrates exactly the principles of the first two metaphors mentioned above. He removes himself from the realm of the common person; he chooses willfully to "go to Innisfree." He goes *now*, immediately. As an exotic, he builds himself an alternative reality of "clay and wattles." Anyone who knows this poem likely knows the story of its inception.[5] Consequently, we also understand that the Innisfree he goes to is the imagined Innisfree, not the physical one. The man is still in London. However, once he moves to the island of his imagination, he discovers the beauty he has searched for:

> I shall have some peace there, for peace comes dropping slow,
> Dropping from the veils of the morning to where the cricket sings;
> There midnight's all a glimmer, and noon a purple glow,
> And evening full of the linnet's wings.

His vision does not fail him, for the island's beauty is eternal in the mind's eye. Finally, and significantly, the hero accepts an increase of burden. This occurs in the last quatrain:

> I will arise and go now, for always night and day
> I hear lake water lapping with low sounds by the shore;
> While I stand on the roadway, or on the pavements grey,
> I hear it in the deep heart's core.

While the poet is able to transcend his physical world, enjoining himself to the paradisiacal island, he is unable to separate himself from the physical world. He, therefore, stands in two worlds: "on the roadway, or on the pavements grey." He partakes of joy in the one and accepts heroically the tragedy of the other. There is no more perfect a way to live.

It might be tempting to call this an escapist poem. However, doing so would be misuse of the word *escape*. It would also be failure to understand the heroic stance Yeats is taking. Any time the poet pulls away from the physical world, he actually embraces it more fully than before. Yeats is not escaping one thing in favor of something else, as Byrd suggested:

> Yeats is using the west of Ireland in the true sense of the pastoral: if the word *escape* is to be applied to Yeats at all, it must be used in the context of an escape *from* London and all the metropolis represents, and an escape *to* the true realities found in more remote, less industrialized areas. (15)

Rather, "The Lake Isle of Innisfree" illustrates conclusively how we may carry paradise and joy with us at all times.

Even "The Stolen Child," one of Yeats's best early poems, draws together some of the same metaphorical elements. The poem invokes the paradisiacal surroundings. These seem attractive to the poetic imagination because the poet's sensibilities make the place better than the real world. Consider these lines:

> Where dips the rocky highland
> Of Sleuth Wood in the lake,
> There lies a leafy island
> Where flapping herons wake
> The drowsy water-rats;
> There we've hid our faery vats,
> Full of berries
> And of the reddest stolen cherries.

This initial description is followed by an invitation extended to humanity, which the poet compares to child-like innocence:

> *Come away, O human child!*
> *To the waters and the wild*
> *With a faery, hand in hand,*
> *For the world's more full of weeping than you can understand.*

The persona bids humanity to leave the world for fairyland—a land outside time, of the imagination. The island possesses serene advantages. There, "We foot it all the night, / Weaving olden dances," "Mingling hands and mingling glances," and leaping and chasing "the frothy bubbles." Elsewhere, "the world is full of troubles / And is anxious in its sleep." After two more invocations from the fairy voice, and another stanza devoted to the charms of the island, the child leaves with the fairies:

> Away with us he's going,
> The solemn-eyed:
> He'll hear no more the lowing
> Of the calves on the warm hillside
> Or the kettle on the hob
> Sing peace into his breast,
> Or see the brown mice bob
> Round and round the oatmeal-chest.

Just as the cherries are stolen in the first stanza, the child is stolen in the last stanza. He seems to go willingly, but one has to wonder. The metaphorical balance struck between cherries and child suggests otherwise: the fruit is equivalent to the child. The comparison is simple enough. The fruit is sweet and good; the child is innocent, and this innocence is implicitly good. However, more crucial and critically delicate are the implicit comparisons. Cherries are stolen from their boughs. Obviously, once the fruit is removed from its nurturing boughs, it cannot grow and it will quickly spoil. However, even if the cherries were allowed to remain on the tree, they would still fall and rot. Regardless their removal from their environment, decay cannot be prevented. Similarly, the child is coaxed deliberately from his nurturing environment. If the pattern runs true, the childlike qualities will spoil from lack of the "warm hillside," the "lowing / Of the calves," "the kettle on the hob." He joins the fairies, but the child undergoes an emotional, mental change. He is "solemn-eyed." One might assume this results from the "world more full of weeping than he can understand." Though he has not yet discovered the ills of this world, the child cannot escape the natural pattern of decay. His "solemn-eyed" countenance illustrates that. Thus, the equivalence of cherries to child also makes an equivalence between the real and the imagined world: one, by and large, is not much better or worse than the other. The restrictions of mortality attend humanity in either realm. Of significance here is what Yeats does with the metaphor of the artist and of the ideal and imagined world. Through these, Yeats provides an alternative view of reality. The artist must work in isolation, and the artist must aspire toward the imagined locale. However, isolation and the paradisiacal island may be detrimental because the artist is drawn from what must ultimately nurture him.

This particular point is reiterated in "The Meditation of the Old Fisherman."

In this poem, the persona speaks negatively about the very things he should find paradisiacal:

> You waves, though you dance by my feet like children at play,
> Though you glow and you glance, though you purr and you dart;
> In the Junes that were warmer than these are, the waves were more gay,
> *When I was a boy with never a crack in my heart.*

Even though the artistic imagination seeks the solitude of the island metaphor, something in the metaphor fails. The fisherman's perception of the world changes, just as his metaphor of the waves changes from human to cat. The ocean itself is immutable though human perception is not; consequently, the poet knows the metaphor of youth does not keep pace with worldly human disintegration. While it is good to dream, the dream requires something of the mutable world. The artifice of the island by itself, then, is simply insufficient. The irony of paradise is its imperfection. Ironic, too, is the poet's desire to reconcile the imperfection of perfect world to the perfect qualities of the imperfect one. Although the island metaphor provides Yeats a starting place for his impossible quest, it is nonetheless a metaphor that examines without resolving the antithetical tensions.

In *The Rose,* Yeats tries to resolve this dilemma by not only retaining the metaphor of the artist in isolation and the island metaphors, but by coupling these to something symbolically permanent rather than impermanent. Here, then, is the third conceptual metaphor of the early poems: Beauty is eternal. In *The Rose*, Yeats leaves the temporal paradise for the paradise established in Irish mythology. The island metaphor remains, but in many of these poems the island is specifically Ireland. To signify the attributes of Ireland, Yeats invokes the symbol of the Rose.

For example, look at "To the Rose upon the Rood of Time":

> *Red Rose, proud Rose, sad Rose of all my days!*
> *Come near me, while I sing the ancient ways:*
> *Cuchulain battling with the bitter tide;*
> *The Druid, grey, wood-nurtured, quiet-eyed,*
> *Who cast round Fergus dreams, and ruin untold;*
> *And thine own sadness, whereof stars, grown old*
> *In dancing silver-sandalled on the sea,*
> *Sing in their high and lonely melody.*
> *Come near, that no more blinded by man's fate,*
> *I find under the boughs of love and hate,*
> *In all poor foolish things that live a day,*
> *Eternal beauty wandering on her way.*

The Rose becomes, for Yeats, a metaphor that incorporates all the concepts of his first collection. It builds upon the metaphors noted above, yet encompasses more because of its flexibility. The poetic temperament leads the artist from the world; it seeks its isolation in an imaginative reality. Still, these are insufficient.

The Rose metaphor defines to a degree what else is necessary. As Bachchan notes, "The Rose is a very old symbol, and . . . has been used again and again by poets to suggest both physical beauty and spiritual purity" (106). Hence, Yeats seeks out more intently not only the beauty of reality and imagined reality, but spiritual reality. Yeats apparently believes spirit is partly cultural, for he embeds spiritual concerns in Irish heritage. He names Irish heroes—Cuchulain and Fergus, and calls to memory the druid spirit of the nation. When he writes, "I find under the boughs of love and hate, / In all poor foolish things that live a day, / Eternal beauty wandering on her way," Yeats positions himself in the middle territory of his previous metaphors. He is on the island, but the island is shaped by both real events and history, and by the poet's recreative, imaginative treatment of the island's materials and mythologies. The island is simultaneously "love and hate," "battling" and "lonely" and beautiful.

To borrow a cliché, the poet puts one of his feet in Ireland's heaven and the other in its hell. A tenuous position, surely, but it realistically reconciles elements of the real and imagined worlds. This way, the poet can occupy the physical Ireland while the poet's mind occupies the imagined fairyland. As Peter Smith explains, "This fairyland . . . is neither life nor death, but a state beyond both . . . .This is the eternal realm of art, which appears much later in 'Byzantium'" (203). Now the artist is able to attain either world at their individual extremes; he can deal with them simultaneously or exclusively, or with any point in the middle-territory. The artist's designs, then, become something of an elaborate spider web.[6] Primary, intersecting strands are extended across a space between two different branches, and a mosaic of additional strands is laid across the primary ones. Innumerable bridges exist, and it is impossible to touch any one part of the web without sending vibrations throughout the rest. Similarly, if some force breaks any strand, the resultant disaster would ruin the entire system. Metaphorically, this is the failure of civilization. So long as the aesthetic design holds together, so does culture. *The Rose* is the germination of Yeats's later metaphors as well as his principle of the gyres. As Smith discusses,

> The end of one cycle, of course, is the beginning of another, when the door of perception will be cleansed. But the new cycle too must undergo its own decline. Or vision will fall and fall again, but for a moment perhaps it will be capable of facing the Rose. Only such a hope will justify Yeats's insistence that the Rose must be sought out and his contempt for those who will not seek her. (197)

Thus, even in the Rose poems, Yeats does the groundwork for "Byzantium." Numerous poetic contrivances, symbols, and metaphors will "fall and fall again," but all in quest of the beauty and spiritual perfection of the Rose.

Smith adds, "Those who seek the vision nonetheless have their choice of many roads. The three royal roads are the subject of a trilogy of poems, 'The Rose of the World,' 'The Rose of Peace,' and 'The Rose of Battle'" (188). In these, spiritual perfection and beauty come upon the roads of the world, of peace, and of battle. The voices of these three poems are all one voice and, concurrently, many. The voice of "The Rose of the World" is wisdom, setting wrong thought right. The voice of wisdom asks, "Who dreamed that beauty passes like a dream?" Beauty, though it appears to dissolve, is actually unalterable. "Troy passed away in one high funeral gleam" because of the Rose's "red lips"; "Usna's children died." The beauty of specific things may die, yet there is always beauty. If we possess wisdom, we can see its existence, in things tangible and in things remembered. What really passes away is "the labouring world" of humanity. Beauty does not exist there. The world craves beauty and destroys for it, and, ironically, destroys the beauty it craves. Because our souls "waver and give place," because the world is a "lonely face," we perceive incorrectly that beauty passes away. However, beauty is constant. Even before the creation of the archangels, who live in a "dim abode" compared to beauty, beauty was omnipresent.

In "The Cold Heaven," wisdom occurs because of the "wavering" of the persona's soul. Beauty's permanence is discovered because of the repudiation of accepted belief systems. In a sublime flash, an instance of transport, what the persona of "The Cold Heaven" experiences is a vision. He describes what he saw: "Suddenly I saw the cold and rook-delighting heaven / That seemed as though ice burned and was but the more ice." Although heaven is first the sky, one cannot overlook the theological connotations. Ironically, the Heaven of this poem is equivalent to the cold Hell of Celtic mythology. Consequently, Heaven, as it is pictured here, is obviously not conventional Heaven. It is cold, it delights the rooks. How is this possible? Heaven allows death, and death feeds the crows. Heaven also kills the "holy tree" ("The Two Trees"), the pure and uncorrupted aesthetic vision where the ideal world can exist. The vision leads the poet to understanding:

> thereupon imagination and heart were driven
> So wild that every casual thought of that and this
> Vanished, and left but memories, that should be out of season
> With the hot blood of youth, of love crossed long ago;
> And I took all the blame out of all sense and reason,
> Until I cried and trembled and rocked to and fro,
> Riddled with light.

The vision annihilates "every casual thought" and brings to surface the memories that have troubled the persona and eradicates blame. This leaves the visionary man "riddled with light." While this seems to be the weeping ecstasy of revelation, *riddled* does not connote *washed*. Rather, the persona is both pierced through and puzzled with light. What is dead in the man is resurrected. However, his revived ghost is "stricken / By the injustice of the skies for punishment." If Heaven is a cold, crow-feeding realm, the king of such a Heaven cannot understand joy, let alone be judicious enough to accept the joy that invalidates Heaven. Hence, when one heaven is discovered, another heaven is destroyed. Of course, Yeats knows joy bears a degree of tragedy. Such knowledge is exemplary of wisdom and heroism.

In "The Rose of Peace," a poem heavily influenced by Blake, the persona speaks with spiritual wisdom. If the Rose of Peace is attained, Heaven and Hell could be reconciled and the archangel Michael would brood "no more upon God's wars."[7] Instead, all "would come at last to God's great town,"

> And God would bid His warfare cease,
> Saying all things were well;
> And softly make a rosy peace,
> A peace of Heaven with Hell.

The juxtapositioning of antithethical heaven against hell is one of those balances Yeats will attempt throughout his mature poetry. Tension exists naturally between these extremities, but a calm and a harmony ensue if the Rose of Peace controls. Spiritual perfection and beauty ensue.

In "The Rose of Battle," the Rose of all Roses has

> come where the dim tides are hurled
> Upon the wharves of sorrow, and heard ring
> The bell that calls us on; the sweet far thing.
> Beauty grown sad with its eternity
> Made you of us, and of the dim grey sea.
> Our long ships loose thought-woven sails and wait,
> For God has bid them share an equal fate;
> And when at last, defeated in His wars,
> They have gone down under the same white stars,
> We shall no longer hear the little cry
> Of our sad hearts, that may not live nor die.

Even in times of war, the Rose is present, perfect and beautiful, waiting for humanity to recognize her presence. However, humanity is lost upon the "dim tides."[8] "Our long ships" are lifetimes which "loose thought-woven sails." Life is "hurled / Upon the wharves of sorrow." While all this transpires, the Rose attends humanity, yet humanity is "defeated."

This is the dilemma of the Rose poems: humanity is defeated because it loses the Rose's perfect beauty and spirit in its quest for the Rose. It attends us always, within close reach, but humanity's failings make the Rose unattainable. Failure is often a prelude to escapism in literature. However, this is not quite the case in Yeats's poetry. Redefinition of this notion comprises the fourth metaphorical concept: escape is really embrace. Any time a hero seeks to escape his or her burden, he or she embraces more. A tragic and joyful occurrence, the individual who understands this and assumes the responsibility is heroic. This concept especially occurs in Yeats's poems about Cuchulain and Fergus. Smith says, "The sense of alienation induced by failure to attain the Rose may expand to cosmic proportions, to a perception of the universe as meaningless. . . . This perception is one to which Fergus is particularly prone. It is part and parcel of his aimless dissatisfaction" (201). While Smith's comment brings Yeats too close to existentialism, the cosmic dilemma is worth noting in the Fergus pieces.

Let us look, first, at portions of "Fergus and the Druid." Fergus is speaking to the Druid, obsessed that the Druid has

> changed and flowed from shape to shape,
> First as a raven on whose ancient wings
> Scarcely a feather lingered, then you seemed
> A weasel moving on from stone to stone,
> And now at last you wear a human shape, . . .

Fergus desires the Druid's miraculous powers. He wants to "cast away" his sorrow; he tells the Druid he would like to "be no more a king / But learn the dreaming wisdom" that belongs to the Druid. When the Druid gives Fergus his "little bag of dreams," Fergus sees his

> life go drifting like a river
> From change to change; I have been many things—
> A green drop in the surge, a gleam of light
> Upon a sword, a fir-tree on a hill,
> An old slave grinding at a heavy quern,
> A king sitting upon a chair of gold
> And all these things were wonderful and great;
> But now I have grown nothing, knowing all.

The grammatical equivalences are worth noting here. Fergus catalogues the "many things" he has been. This catalogue may be charted as follows:

Noun-phrase	Preposition	Object of the Preposition
a green drop	in	the surge
a gleam of light	upon	a sword
a fir-tree	on	a hill
an old slave grinding	at	a heavy quern
a king sitting	upon	a chair of gold

Interestingly, the noun-phrases move downward, from abstract to concrete; that is, those at the bottom of the chart are more tangible than those at the top. If the reductive pattern is metaphorically consistent, the king is the most concrete and least desirable form due to its proximity to "nothing." Once Fergus knows all, he is trapped in "great webs of sorrow."[9]

Compare this to "Who Goes with Fergus?" In this poem, the yoke Fergus bears has not been lifted, though it seems clearly lightened. Yeats writes, "brood on hopes and fear no more" and "no more turn aside and brood / Upon love's bitter mystery." For now, Fergus is exultant in the burden of his wisdom:

> For Fergus rules the brazen cars,
> And rules the shadows of the wood,
> And the white breast of the dim sea
> And all dishevelled wandering stars.

As Byrd points out, "In the first poem Fergus has given up an unsatisfactory life for an existence of sorrow—Fergus sees his fate as a dreamy, futile martyrdom" (49). A transformation occurs when we rediscover Fergus in the second poem. Byrd continues: "[Fergus] has gone through a poetic dark night of the soul to emerge in the light of true poetic being. He is no longer on the rim of the sea: he rules the white breast of the sea. He is not only in the center of life: he controls it" (49). The hero is able to transcend despair and sorrow by his assertion of power over the world; he immerses himself into its fury and controls it. Fergus, then, links together the metaphors Yeats has constructed all along. The contemplative person, one with an aesthetic imagination, desires departure from the real world. However, right in the midst of escape, the individual plunges hopelessly, wondrously, and joyously into existence the individual masters. Byrd contends that

> the two poems on Fergus show the inner progress of the developing poet, from the physical world of appearance, the so-called "real world," to the true world of ideal existence. Again, Yeats has not tried to escape

> life. With Fergus he enters life, the eternal world of poetic reality. (49)

Despite what many writers state, Yeats never tries to escape life. He initiates any number of distancings, he retreats, he annihilates what he perceives is the real world. However, these always bring him irrevocably back upon the real world. He always finds his feet planted in different realms; his mind's eye sees clearly the ideal made possible by both worlds. The poet, like Fergus, never escapes "into a state of tranquillity"; rather, he takes "on a greater burden. . . . He has not rejected this world; he has accepted more than this world" (Byrd 71).

What the poet ultimately accepts is the burden of knowlege. The poet must know the world better than unreflecting humanity can. First, the average human could never imagine, let alone accept, the burden of an all encompassing vision. Yeats does much the same as Cuchulain when that hero fights the sea. It might be remembered, first, that "Cuchulain's Fight with the Sea" follows "Fergus and the Druid." As Bachchan says, "It appears that [Yeats] wanted to oppose Fergus, the man of dreams, with Cuchulain, the man of the sword" (51). By doing so, Yeats creates a metaphorical balance between both men; somehow their tasks are equal. Both pursue the elusive ideal existence, just as much as Yeats pursues the elusive poetic ideal. Fergus and Cuchulain are antithetical, as much in Yeats's poetry is. Antithesis helps the poet to find, through his metaphors, what he would later call "tragic joy" ("The Gyres"). This antithetical unity becomes the poet's chore. As Emer says in "Cuchulain Fights with the Sea," "It is not meet / To idle life away, a common herd." Unlike the beast of common, idling humanity, Yeats endeavors to make sense of his life.

Key concerns arise in "Cuchulain Fights with the Sea." Emer sends her son to meet with Cuchulain; she instructs him to tell his "name and lineage to him / Whose blade compels, and wait till they have found / Some feasting man that the same oath has bound." This, the boy, who is "mighty Cuchulain's son," does. However, the challenge starts a fight, and the boy's father kills his own son before he knows his identity. Smith says, "Cuchulain, the violent man, is...forced to recognize a meaningless universe. The moral of 'Cuchulain Fights with the Sea' is that the violent man cannot hope to attain the Rose because violence is self-defeating" (202). I agree with Smith in part. Granted, the man is forced to recognize the nonsense of existence, as exemplified in the misplaced oath of honor and the subsequent battle between father and son. I agree that Cuchulain defeats himself, for the son is his mirror-image. However, I hesitate to embrace any criticism so neatly categorized as a "moral." Rather, Yeats gives us an illustration of both cosmic or self-defeating nonsense while simultaneously asserting the irony of the Rose quest. This nonsense and its violence keeps us from finding the Rose, yet it is also a path to the Rose. To live, one must die.[10] This is a literal though antithetical truth. Metaphorically, however, the human ego must die before humanity can progress to the ideal realm. After the Druids "chaunted for three days," Cuchulain is left fighting with the "invulnerable tide." In perpetuity, Cuchulain fights his losing battle. Despite its futility, he fights nonetheless and fights forever. This is a heroic gesture. Another mirror, the tide is invulnerable as is Cuchulain. As these are invulnerable, so is the persistent poetic sensibility that chooses the burden of existence.

Aengus, from "The Song of Wandering Aengus," is also a contemplative man; searching for the ideal perfection of the world, Aengus begins his song:

> I went out to the hazel wood,
> Because a fire was in my head,
> And cut and peeled a hazel wand,
> And hooked a berry to a thread;
> And when white moths were on the wing,
> And moth-like stars were flickering out,
> I dropped the berry in a stream,
> And caught a little silver trout.

Many of the same metaphorical patterns occur here that occurred in the poems already discussed. Humanity willfully removes itself to an alternative reality. In this poem, reality is not an island location. However, the stream embankment is at least related. The repose is necessary to sooth the "fire" in Aengus's head. This fire is equivalent to the anguish occupying Cuchulain's mind when "with head bowed on his knees Cuchulain stayed." Certainly, the circumstances are not equal: one man is in violent turmoil; the other's troubles are minor by comparison. The philosophical, aesthetic problems of making sense of the universe, however, are equivalent. Furthermore, Yeats introduces yet another metaphor. The man in retreat "to the hazel wood" is nothing other than a public man seeking privacy. Many of Yeats's poems study this dilemma, as in the image of the "smiling public man" of "Among School Children."

When Aengus returns home with the trout he has caught, the vision occurs. The mingling of the real and ideal worlds forces the experience. Consider this particular stanza of "The Song of Wandering Aengus":

> When I had laid it on the floor
> I went to blow the fire aflame,
> But something rustled on the floor,
> And someone called me by my name:
> It had become a glimmering girl
> With apple blossom in her hair
> Who called me by my name and ran

And faded through the brightening air.

The vision is sublime, much akin to the Romantic tradition of Byron.[11] When the "glimmering girl" fades "through the brightening air," the persona understands the extreme significance of the lost vision. At the moment of transport, he discovers the need for the ideal—the Rose. And, as soon as he discovers it, he loses it. Zwerdling writes,

> Aengus spends the rest of his life in a fruitless search to recapture the lost vision . . . . Yeats's visionary, then, like all his other heroic men, is not a success but a failure, and it is only through the transcendence of that failure and the despair which it might bring that he becomes truly heroic. (177)

Zwerdling's final point is vital to a study of Yeats's poetry. Granted, the endeavor of vision-seeking may at best fail, but the search nonetheless successfully brings about transcendence of failure and despair. The "common herd's" efforts would cease with failure; the heroic individual, on the other hand, searches after islands and visions, sees them fade, yet wanders on—as Aengus does, as Yeats does.

Yeats asserts much the same notion in "Into the Twilight":

Out-worn heart, in a time out-worn,
Come clear of the nets of wrong and right;
Laugh, heart, again in the grey twilight,
Sigh, heart, again in the dew of the morn.

This seems to be what Yeats is looking for, the discernment that existence expects acceptance of extremities of right and wrong. Such acceptance, however, only provides for us "out-worn" hearts; time passes and our getting caught up in the nets becomes even the more futile. Better for our hearts to laugh and sigh in both the morning and the twilight. Yeats reiterates these sentiments later on when he writes "there's more enterprise / In walking naked" ("A Coat").

To examine the entrapments of "wrong and right," we need only to look at a few other poems from *The Wind Among the Reeds*. In "The Song of the Old Mother," the "wrong and right" nets, the "out-worn heart," the "time out-worn," and the twilight and morning are repeated. The persona is the old woman herself, complaining about how burdensome her life has become:

I rise in the dawn, and I kneel and blow
Till the seed of the fire flicker and glow;
And then I must scrub and bake and sweep

Till stars are beginning to blink and peep;
And the young lie long and dream in their bed
Of the matching of ribbons for bosom and head,
And their day goes over in idleness,
And they sigh if the wind but lift a tress:
While I must work because I am old,
And the seed of the fire gets feeble and cold.

This poem is composed of antithetical mirrors. The reflection is not only a reversal of the image but a paradoxical alteration of the image. The old mother perceives herself against the image of her children: she works hard, the children do nothing; she is old, the children are young; she rises early, the children sleep; she has worries, the children are carefree. Even the structure of the poem is built upon antithesis: the opening lines illustrate the kindling of the fire, but the closing line illustrates how that fire is going out. The structure metaphorically suits this notion, too: the fire *growing* is given two lines; the fire *dying* is reduced to one. Metaphorically, the "seed of the fire" is simultaneously the youth and vitality of the children, and the old mother's passion for life is a dying ember. Like kindling waiting to be consumed by flames, the children are in their beds, dreaming, awaiting a spark. Like the fire at night, the old woman awaits her own demise. The poem is very well-crafted. If the title of the *Crossways* collection indicates subjects crisscrossing, this poem reinforces this concept ten years later. For every cross Yeats makes, the nets of "wrong and right" become increasingly more binding. The woman, because she is trapped in the network, cannot escape the bitterness she feels toward youth and toward her own hard life.

I have already discussed Yeats's concept of beauty's perpetual existence. "The Old Men Admiring Themselves in the Water" seems antithetical to that concept, however:

I heard the old, old men say,
'Everything alters,
And one by one we drop away.'
They had hands like claws, and their knees
Were twisted like old-thorn trees
By the waters.
I heard the old, old men say,
'All that's beautiful drifts away
Like the waters.'

First, Yeats compares the old men to beast and gnarled vegetation. The claw imagery, doubtlessly, brings to mind the beast and bird imagery that occupies the later poetry; the animalization is vital to his later metaphors. Furthermore, the reverse personification of the men's knees is essential to note, for here the poet experiments with humanity in forms other than human, as he does in the "Byzantium" poems. Worth notice, too, is the irony of the title-word, *admiring*. To *admire* is to find something appealing in the observation. Even though the men are "rough-beasts," so to speak, they apparently find something admirable in their reflections.[12] This undercuts the final line. Though they acknowledge their images, they fail to recognize the image as beautiful. Incorrectly, the old men assume beauty is equal to youthful physique. The poet, however, illustrates once again that beauty is intact in perception, in the imagination.

Compare this to "The Two Trees." In this poem, as Smith says, "The full of human vision and the offence of the reason against the imagination are dealt with schematically" (197). The very first lines,

> Beloved, gaze in thine own heart,
> The holy tree is growing there;
> From joy the holy branches start,
> And all the trembling flowers they bear,

bring to mind "The Song of the Happy Shepherd." Beauty exists in the imagination, in the individual's heart. The "holy tree" is nothing other than wisdom which understands instantly the value of imaginative reality as opposed to physical reality. The "holy tree" is equivalent to "the great-rooted blossomer" of "Among School Children." Furthermore, among the leaves of the tree,

> There the Loves a circle go,
> The flaming circle of our days,
> Gyring, spiring to and fro
> In those great ignorant leafy ways; . . .

Here, Yeats is working out the origin of his system of spirals, for the gyres of the "holy tree" are also those that shape the metaphor of the world. He has moved beyond the mere network of "wrong and right." Rather, this is a freely spinning network—we are caught in its current, ignorantly, innocently, flaming in Love. Therefore, the poet tells us:

> Gaze no more in the bitter glass
> The demons, with their subtle guile,
> Lift up before us when they pass,
> Or only gaze a little while;
> For there a fatal image grows
> That the stormy night receives,

Roots half hidden under snows,
Broken boughs and blackened leaves.

The warning brings to mind the image of the old men admiring themselves. Instead of seeing where beauty exists, too often humanity responds to its reflection in bitterness. The "fatal image" destroys the "holy tree," giving rise instead to "ravens of unresting thought."[13]

The visionary experience, however, of the engaged imagination allows us to ignore the lies we perceive in our mirrors. It allows us to be heroic. Heroism is why we pursue the Rose, for Beauty exists and awaits us where the many roads cross. It is why Fergus accepts his greater burden, why Cuchulain fights the sea, why Heaven is an icy reflection shattered by sublime revelation. The metaphorical patterns of these early poems lead overwhelmingly to those Yeats wrote later.

Thus far, I have noted these particular conceptual metaphors:

One, the aesthetic individual is a wandering hero. The hero stands apart from the "common herd." An outsider, an exotic, the hero is a visionary, able to live simultaneously in the physical realm and the imaginary worlds.

Two, Paradise is an island in the imagination. Reality is not the physical world alone, nor is it the longed for mythic worlds of Eden or Heaven. Reality is a reconcilement of the physical and mythic, a Paradise constructed in the mind and heart.

Three, beauty is eternal. It does not decay or die. Always attainable, faulty perception makes it unattainable.

Four, escape is embrace. Any time a hero seeks to escape life's burden the hero embraces more. This is both tragic and joyful. The individual who understands this and assumes the responsibility is heroic.

Through these metaphors, Yeats constructs a building of poetry, word by word, making for himself what Heaven, what philosophy and belief-systems cannot provide. He constructs his alternative reality, where one can be a hero in a world that "weighed so lightly what" its heroes gave ("September 1913"). The hero moves from despair into antithetical joy and increased responsibility.

Chapter 3

Anima Bruta: Yeats's Metaphors of Blood and Beast

In the early poems, Yeats experiments with fairyland as the beginnings of his world of artifice. He cannot quite secure that world despite the efforts of his wandering heroes, despite the embrace of the imaginative islands, despite the burdenous joy, without also embracing characteristics that seem contradictory to the "higher" order of humanity. In some of Yeats's most compelling poems, the human creature is an unfinished one, out of place, unsatisfied, and incapable of achieving spiritual and intellectual perfection. The human creature may aspire toward reason and detached contemplation; it may reason a path to kindness, mercy, sympathy, and civilization. However, the indisputable fact is the fallibility of emotion and intelligence, especially when humanity's animal nature is repressed. Because the human creature is controlled in part by blood and instinct, its beastliness makes the concept of "higher" humanity impossible. Pursuit of the high ideals of the "humane" makes humankind a weak species. Similarly, pursuit of God makes humankind impotent, for power and wisdom cannot spring from where there is nothing.

Yeats begins to understand the conflict between the duality of human nature fairly well by the time he begins writing such poems as "The White Birds," "The Withering of the Boughs," and the beggar poems.[1] These poems address the impossibility of attaining paradise permanently in this world or elsewhere, and the ensuing tug of war existent between one disillusioning circumstance and, likely, what would be another. For example, in "The White Birds," the human protagonist is accutely aware of how "the flame of the blue star of twilight" "has awaked in our hearts . . . a sadness that may not die." He assumes that being a white bird riding "on the wandering foam" is more enviable than being human. The birds seem carefree, unlike the humans whose implicit burdens create such futile desires. The physical world is oppressive, while the *dreamed-of* world seems more lasting and liberating. While the concept of transmutation belongs to Romance, the realist and skeptic recognize immediately the ludicrousness of self-pity and foolish desire. After all, the speaker is already *animal*; his myopicism creates the unnecessary hopelessness. The pattern that illustrates dissatisfied humanity as desiring either an alternative world or an alternative physicality becomes essential to Yeat's poetic redesigning of the world. In this pattern, the human creature often sees something more vital in the non-human or animal world.

In other pieces, the conflict Yeats scrutinizes has to do with the duality of desire itself. The human creature is not satisfied with what it has; it desires more and gains nothing. Consider, for example, the irony of the personification of the old crane in "The Three Beggars." The old crane mutters, "I have not found a thing to eat, / For only rubbish comes my way." His attitude is juxtaposed to the beggars' desire for money. King Guaire's question, "Do men who least desire get most, / Or get the most who most desire?" prompts a wager the beggars cannot hope to win. King Guaire will award a thousand pounds to the beggar who sleeps first, within three days. Each man desires the wealth so much that "none closed his blood-shot eyes but sought / to keep his fellows from their sleep." Consequently, they "mauled and bit" like animals until the wager period was expended and no one man won. Simultaneously, all three "fell down upon the dust and snored," as if contentment only comes from sleep. The heron Yeats had left standing in the rushes in the first stanza remarks: "And maybe I shall take a trout / If but I do not seem to care." The bird wants a trout; the king wants wisdom as it pertains to desire; the beggars want money. All discover, perhaps, that those who desire most get nothing. Passions become too intense, too unnatural, and the result of misplaced passions—blood impulses for something not blood—is that we end up in "the dust." Surely, the reference to dust is equally a reference to death. Contentment also comes from learning to be still, accepting the totality of the individual circumstance. The dissatisfied human will forever be "running to Paradise" ("Running to Paradise"), yet miss the paradise of resolved antinomies.

These poems, among others, shape a directional change for Yeats's poetry. Where the early poems illustrate a wandering hero's pursuit of island paradises, and how escape is actually an embrace of greater burden, Yeats's pursuit of paradise in the shape of poetry burdens him with the re-creation of his personal universe. As Albright says, "Yeats's heaven, according to *A*

Vision, is the place where all antinomies are resolved, the gyres turned into a sphere" (118). However, Yeats's heaven is self-made. Asserting his own procreative powers, he exercises both the human and the divine traits of power and wisdom. Simultaneously, he accepts the existence of his own fleshliness, his own animalism. Thus, he understands more fully antinomies of reason and instinct that war for dominance within the human creature. Part of the procreative dance of poetry, then, is to find paradise through the resolution of these antinomies. To desire either extreme is an impotent desire; to desire both is wisdom and potency.

These particular concepts lead to Yeats's submersion into the "passionate intensity" of blood, beast, and sexual metaphors. In the design of what I term the *anima bruta* metaphor, Yeats constructs many of his best poems.[2] *Anima bruta* suggests the intertwined character Yeats illustrates in these particular poems. *Anima*, the soul or life principle, implies the high ideals of humanity; this is juxtaposed to *bruta*, the animal or the brute, the passionate or the violent. The higher aspirations of the "humane" make humans too bloodless; as Yeats describes in "Adam's Curse," to love "in the old high way" is equivalent to all those fine things that "needs much labouring." The "fine things" make us grow "as weary-hearted as that hollow moon," turning us into an empty shell. Elevated emotions deny us the flesh and blood of our existence. Without this, life becomes flaccid.

The use of *flaccid* is an intended sexual reference because it complements Yeats's use of the sexual imagery found in the poems constructed from the anima bruta metaphor. This imagery suggests the distinction Yeats sees between the impotent and the potent life. As Allen Grossman notes, "Throughout his life Yeats meditated on the sexual act, on the fearful apocalyptic consequences of birth, and, under the symbolism of coitus and birth, on the problem of poetry" (55). The anima bruta metaphor addresses these particulars, and enchances the poetry with an indelible wash of passion that did not so often attend the early poems. However, this passion is problematic in its extreme: a creature that is all animal tends to be blood-thirsty, untamed, violent. Potency at its extreme is brutish passion, incapable of romance or love. The anima bruta metaphor examines the polarities while it suggests the human ideal exists between the poles.

To understand more clearly what the desired place is, Yeats must dislocate his protagonists into variable circumstances and into other, non-human shapes. If the result of the experiment is positive, we discover nearer perfection through the resolve of the extremes. If the result is negative, we witness the impotency and emptiness of humanity. In one instance, the anima bruta metaphor may examine how the dual characteristics of human nature interact in romantic situations. Another poem may illustrate the metaphor at its most animal extreme. Yet another may fuse characteristics of humane and animal natures. Significantly, the anima bruta metaphor allows us to view the antinomies of emotional and intellectual humanity and physical, sexual and violent humanity. The juxtaposition of these extremities lets Yeats redefine humanity and lets us rethink the way we perceive the human place in the world.

As noted previously, sexual imagery is important to the anima bruta metaphor. Even in the originary poems, the importance of this imagery is worth noting because it suggests the power or potency too contemplative humanity seems to lack. In "The White Birds," for example, the longing for the alternative reality carries passion along with the body in transmutation, as illustrated by "the wandering foam." The sea is both the beginning and the end of life; the sea is mystery; it is the ovum of the world, and the "wandering foam" is simultaneously rabid passion as much as it is ejaculate. The sex act is a concurrent spasm of birth and death, as is the transport from the physical to the imaginative reality. Because it is both birth and death, physical and imaginative, the one extreme cannot exclude the other.

Even in the poem "In the Seven Woods," illustrating how Yeats had gone to Lady Gregory's home at Coole to calm his nerves following his emotionally destructive relationship to Maud Gonne, the sexual imagery is evident. Consider the following passage:

> I have heard the pigeons of the Seven Woods
> Make their faint thunder, and the garden bees
> Hum in the lime-tree flowers; and put away
> The unavailing outcries and the old bitterness
> That empty the heart.

Transport to serenity occurs through sensual behavior, the "faint thunder" of the pigeons (which thunder most during their mating dances), and in the hum of the bees as they collect nectar.[3] The poet's assertion, "I am contented, for I know that Quiet / Wanders laughing and eating her wild heart / Among pigeons and bees," suggests the poet's understanding of this; even if he himself is a troubled human, the animal instinct can bring him contentment. Something of the animal, I suspect, is awakened instinctively in the man.

In another early poem, "To Some I have Talked with by the Fire," Yeats writes of "the dark folk who live in souls / Of passionate men, like bats in the dead trees." Take note of the metaphorical equivalences here: the "dark folk . . . in souls" are bats; "passionate men" are "dead trees." Bats, of course, are emblematically blood-creatures.[4] They are, furthermore, winged creatures and flying is a recognized sexual metaphor. These "dark folk" occupy the souls of "passionate men." Humanity cannot be passionate without the soul-possessing creatures of blood. However, Yeats locates the bats in "dead trees," mortal humanity. Without animal presences, the human creature is lifeless. Passion is eternal, but passionate flesh is not.[5] The "twilight companies" "sigh with mingled sorrow and content, / Because their blossoming dreams have never bent / Under the fruit of evil and of good." The "embattled flaming multitude" makes a "rapturous music" "with the clashing of their sword-blades." Even when morning overrides the dark, "the white hush" quiets everything except "the loud beat / Of their long wings, the flash of their white feet." The images are clearly sexual, illustrating, metaphorically, the act of coitus. Everything merges, everything succeeds, everything fails, yet everything creative or procreative in sensual creatures leads toward perfection.

This discussion about sexuality brings to mind Yeats's poem about "Solomon and the Witch." This particular poem illustrates the anima bruta metaphor as it relates to sex in romantic love. Granted, we might give this poem a simple biographical reading and recognize it as a love poem Yeats writes to his wife after the occasion of her automatic writings. As Ellmann discusses it,

> Marriage to Georgie Hyde-Lees released his energies like a spring. He fell deeply in love with his wife and knew for the first time the happiness of a relatively uncomplicated relationship with another person. He was astonished to find himself playing the role of husband and, after February 1919, of father, without feeling that it was a role at all. "The marriage bed," he wrote later, "is the symbol of the solved antinomy." Certainly it was so for him, and the ecstasy of the solution shines through the worldly humor of the poems, "Solomon and the Witch" and "Solomon to Sheba," which he wrote in 1918. A great serenity came over Yeats as he emerged from the isolation and eccentricity of bachelorhood into peace and harmony. His wife was kind and self-sacrificing; she understood his strange mixture of arrogance and diffidence, and behind the pose which he put on before strangers found him deeply human. (*Yeats* 221)

This is a pleasant appraisal of Yeats's regard for his wife and serves to amplify the content of "Solomon and the Witch." Acceptance of this appraisal exclusively, however, might ruin some more important metaphorical points that occur in the poem. Solomon, of course, is the epitome of wise men. In Yeats's poem, however, Solomon has been seduced by the Witch (Sheba)—one wonders who is the wiser.[6] Ellmann, himself, notes how "nothing that had happened to [Yeats] before was more dramatically exciting than the automatic writing of his wife, which he felt put wisdom at last within his reach" (*Yeats* 221). The woman of the poem, and perhaps the woman Yeats was married to, seems to possess an understanding of the duality of humanity that neither Solomon nor Yeats yet possesses. In the women's characters, we sense a subtle instinctual superiority that disarms the men's sense of humane wisdom.

Because of Sheba, excessively erotic things bind the sexual with the spiritual in "Solomon and the Witch." Zwerdling puts it somewhat differently; he says, "Before the word 'ecstasy' became part of the language of the marriage manuals, it was used to describe religious experience" (170). Yeats manipulates both definitions of ecstacy. Sheba speaks:

> 'Last night, where under the wild moon
> On grassy mattress I had laid me,
> Within my arms great Solomon,
> I suddenly cried out in a strange tongue
> Not his, not mine.'

Is this "strange tongue" the voice of orgasmic delight or of ecstatic transport? Both are likely; but, equally likely is that the "strange tongue" is the voice of spirit released at the peak of religious experience.[7] Solomon, as the myth goes, "who understood / Whatever has been said, sighed, sung, / Howled, miau-d, barked, belled, yelled, cried, crowed," responds to the woman allegorically. Her moanings, equivalent to the long list of animal utterances, are interpreted as

> 'A cockerel
> Crew from a blossoming apple bough
> Three hundred years before the Fall,
> And never crew again till now,
> And would not now but that he thought,
> Chance being at one with Choice at last,
> All that the brigand apple brought
> And this foul world were dead at last.
> He that crowed out eternity
> Thought to have crowed it in again. . . .'

The sexual union, then, is interpreted to have been the end of the world's existence and its simultaneous conception. The union of Chance and Choice, of accident and will, is "a single light, / When oil and wick are burned in one." Solomon points out that Choice and Chance are coupled to "cruelties." The sex act, though implicitly creative, is also destructive; Solomon compares it to murder and says that "maybe the bride-bed brings despair." Maybe so, but passions come to us by chance and by choice, as does the consummation of those passions. We submit our bodies to a particular violence, and this violence is equivalent to the eternal death and birth of the universe. When Sheba says, "Yet the world stays," she is exactly right. The sex act annunciates the end and the beginning of something. The world has been crowed in and out, but in such instance as cannot be mortally comprehended. When we live in both the physical and the spiritual worlds, our passions intact, we play out the universal mandalic dance. Yeats completes "Solomon and the Witch" with both a wry and legitimately appropriate response from Sheba:

> 'The night has fallen; not a sound
> In the forbidden sacred grove
> Unless a petal hit the ground,
> Nor any human sight within it
> But the crushed grass where we have lain;
> And the moon is wilder every minute.
> O! Solomon! let us try again.'

She and Solomon, metaphorically, have just destroyed and recreated the world. Wondrously, Chance and Choice have swung round again. The creature of blood must say, "Why not try again?" Where the biographical reading fails with this poem is the fact that Yeats's wife tires of the exhausting physical chore of the automatic writings (Ellmann, *Yeats* 222). However, Sheba is not exhausted here; she wants to keep the blood active.

Zwerdling discusses this attitude somewhat, and an examination of what he has to say may be worthwhile:

> For though the visionary may be able to combine physical life with spiritual truth, though it is true that such experience is within man's scope, the ultimate fruition is still denied to the Yeatsian seer: his 'vision' does not last. We get a sense of this when Sheba, in describing her visionary experience to Solomon, suddenly realizes that it has been nothing but a momentary release from a humdrum existence: 'Yet the world stays.' And here is the basic problem with all of Yeats's visionaries, that, in spite of a momentary fruition, 'the world stays,' and the ordinary conditions of life are reestablished. The very metaphor of sexual union obviously emphasizes the transcience of the experience, but even in poems which do not describe 'ecstasy' in strictly sexual terms, the visionary state is at best a few moments snatched from the immense flow of time . . . ." (176)

Zwerdling is at least partially correct. There is just a momentary fruition; the vision does not last long. However, this should not suggest failure. First, in virtually all traditions, the visionary state is a momentary one; when it is not momentary, it is madness. Second, having the vision is enough if the persona does not despair over the loss of that vision. Chance and Choice may come around again, just as this poem illustrates. The nihilist might experience the vision, realize he or she has been relinguished to the mundane world, and despair to self-destruction. This does not occur in Yeats's poetry. The vision, despite its brevity, always draws us back toward the ecstatic realization that the experience has happened and that the experience can be relived. As Yeats says later in "Vacillation," "I was blessèd and could bless," and, in "A Dialogue of Self and Soul":

> I am content to live it all again
> And yet again, if it be life to pitch
> Into the frog-spawn of a blind man's ditch,
> A blind man battering blind men; . . .

In this particular case, Zwerdling belongs to the species of blind men. The failure of sustained vision is not the failure of vision. That Sheba wants to "try again" is not from her despair at finding the mundane world persists, but that she, passionately enough, wants to relive the blessing of Chance and Choice. Sheba's sentiments are much the same as Yeats's in "A Dialogue of Self and Soul." She, too, is "content to follow to its source / Every event in action" because there

> So great a sweetness flows into the breast
> We must laugh and we must sing,
> We are blest by everything,
> Everything we look upon is blest.

As Tennyson noted in the long elegy "In Memoriam A. H. H." "I have felt."[8] That suffices because feeling or even memory of feeling may return in perpetuity. Thus, if marriage is meant to last for eternity, its longevity must rely in part upon the fusion of romantic love and sexuality. Romantic love belongs to anima, while sexuality belongs to bruta.

Needless to say, "Solomon and the Witch" alludes to the Biblical tale, though thinly—Yeats never endorses Biblical ideology but uses its familiarity to suggest something uncommon or unconventional. The Biblical allusion as metaphor provides him a vehicle for universality while it exclusively deals with individual passion. Often, at such times, the anima bruta metaphor discredits conventional "humane" theology because of its denial of flesh. Similarly, in "The Collar-Bone of a Hare," Yeats reduces the central motif of the allusion to minute proportions to repudiate the stultifying inhibitions of the "humane" world. The opening of "The Collar-bone of a Hare," "Would I could cast a sail on the water," portrays that desire to embrace the distant locales of the imagination. The alternative reality would provide the persona hedonistic glee, what Graham Martin calls "a dreamt-of eternity of youthful love" (63), where he could

> alight at the comely trees and the lawn,
> The playing upon pipes and the dancing,
> And learn that the best thing is
> To change my loves while dancing
> And pay but a kiss for a kiss.

This creates a picture of libertine sexuality, as evidenced in the twice-mentioned dancing and an unrestricted amour. The poet regards this as heroic, though it is not heroic in the Biblical sense.[9] Rather than Samson finding the jawbone of an ass and using it to ward off the Philistines, the poet

> would find by the edge of that water
> The collar-bone of a hare
> Wore thin by the lapping of water,
> And pierce it through with a gimlet and stare
> At the old bitter world where they marry in churches,
> And laugh over the untroubled water
> At all who marry in churches,
> Through the white thin bone of a hare.

The poet does not require superhuman strength nor the heavy ass-bone to defeat what he perceives as the enemy of the good, passionate life. He can do it with the fragile hare's bone.[10] The hole he drills and stares through makes the insignificant world even smaller. Yeats's Philistine army is the church, the enemy of "the untroubled water" of passionate living.

Part of Yeats's trouble with Christianity is its focus upon the dualistic nature of humanity, and the church's rejection of flesh in favor of spirit. Obviously, Yeats would sense the error of any rejection of one part of human nature. The artist values the imagined and ideal world, as well as vital passions. The church's restrictions upon imagination and passion make it an intolerable, troublesome entity, opposed to the very things Yeats values. The Biblical myth is a static myth (God is the same yesterday, today, and tomorrow), and this is destructive.[11] What Yeats favors in "The Collar-bone of a Hare" is the freedom passionate living allows, not the confines of the church.

The anima bruta metaphor examines this notion of freedom in "The Cat and the Moon." The cat is not a restricted creature; "The cat went here and there" while "the moon spun round like a top." The moon itself is a curious emblem: it spins, it goes through its phases, yet it is locked forever in its unalterable orbit. Yeats calls the cat "the nearest kin of the moon," just as man is nearest kin of God. Just as "the pure cold light in the sky / Troubled [the cat's] animal blood," if the moon is a metaphor for God, human blood must also be troubled by God's "pure cold light." Even the meter of these lines creates a metaphor of trouble. Scanned, the following pattern is revealed:

> ˘ ´ ´ ´ ˘ ˘ ´
>
> The pure | cold light | in the sky
>
> ´ ˘ ˘ ´ ˘ ˘ ´
>
> Troubled | his an | imal blood.

The prosody consists of a series of substitutions. The spondee ("cold light") is a departure from the conventional iambic pattern; then, so are the anapests that complete each line and the trochee ("Troubled"). The trochee is especially important, since it is a clear inversion of the iambic pattern; the trochee troubles the meter most.

A significant question arises next, followed by Yeats's proposed revision of God. He asks,

> Do you dance, Minnaloushe, do you dance?
> When two close kindred meet,
> What better than call a dance?
> Maybe the moon may learn,
> Tired of that courtly fashion,
> A new dance turn.

Animal blood dances, for "Minnaloushe runs in the grass / Lifting his delicate feet." The question implies that humanity does not dance with its nearest kin, though, metaphorically, the natural thing is that God and humanity should dance, that God should learn a "new dance turn." "Courtly fashion," however, suggests those high, "humane" ideals belonging to anima alone. If our "sacred moon overhead" takes on a "new phase," just as the cat's eyes "pass from change to change," there might exist a more natural relationship between humanity and its concept of God. However, humanity's curse is its unnatural relationship with its "nearest kin." Like the cat, the human is a changing, animal creature. The cat's moon changes, but our unchangeable God condemns humanity for the passions inherent in his creations.

Of course, being a passionate creature is not always a matter of love, excited joy, or dance. Obviously, the conflicts humanity has with belief systems deprive us of liberation. As well, our contemplative natures can disappoint our passions, too, as is illustrated in "The Wild Swans at Coole." That Yeats sees equivalences between animals and humanity has been discussed previously; also, the metaphorical equivalences between swans and Maud Gonne, and swans and love, were noted in Chapter 1. But if Minnaloushe in "The Cat and the Moon" was "troubled in his animal blood," Yeats in "The Wild Swans at Coole" is troubled in his blood and soul by the too-changing world and body in which he lives. Part of the blessing of being a creature of blood is change; however, change is also a curse. When the swans suddenly fly, they "scatter wheeling in great broken rings." The word *broken* is essential because it belongs to the poet's perception of the flight. He is out of unity with the swans; that animal part in him has been denied the communion of flight. When Yeats writes, "I have looked upon those brilliant creatures, / And now my heart is sore," the soreness results from his realization that he is no longer one of the "brilliant creatures." "All's changed"; "their hearts have not grown old," but his has. Apparently, Yeats views this scene from the vantage point of a man decaying in a decaying world. The vision does not take place in the perfect world of the imagination. Blood-passion, however, can send us joyously from this world into the next. But when those blood-passions are disappointed they land us, earthbound, to the physical world. Furthermore, where the static seemed troublesome in "The Cat and the Moon," here the static seems something desirable. What is desirable, quite clearly, is the seeming eternal love and paradise the swans enjoy in the natural world; humanity cannot share the swan's joy unless vision allows humanity to transcend reality.

Rajan makes an interesting case for "The Wild Swans at Coole." He says the swans "stand for the life-force." However, he also states that the swans "stand for inspiration, building by the lake's edge where the wind blows among the reeds. The poet awakes into reality to find them gone, but perhaps the dream which they inhabit remains at his calling and perhaps the sources of life lie in the dreams of poetry" (108). This seems plausible (though I think the concept is worked out more convincingly in "Among School Children"). At the end of "The Wild Swans at Coole," the poet only wonders who the swans will please when he finds "they have flown away." Despairing, Yeats has no reason to believe they will remain "at his calling"; they are emblems for someone else.

For comparative purposes, let us look at "Among School Children." This poem addresses much the same conflict of the mutable blood-passions. However, this poem illustrates Yeats's ability to transform through intense vision the disappointment into renewed passion. Although I will discuss "Among School Children" more directly, relative to the metaphor of dissolution in Chapter 6, the poem is relevant to the anima bruta metaphor. If Yeats finds himself out of unity in "The Wild Swans at Coole," he works himself back into unity in "Among School Children." The opening stanza shows Yeats out of place, in a role that somehow does not suit him. He is a "questioning," "sixty-year-old smiling public man" in the company of a nun and children. In "The Wild Swans at Coole," the swans were emblematic of continued youthfulness, and this made him heartsick; in "The Collar-bone of a Hare," he levelled the church with a miniscule bone. Obviously, because the opening stanza of this poem places him among youthfulness and the church, he finds himself in territory that would trouble "his animal blood" ("The Cat and the Moon"). Here the troubling of blood is equal to the troubling of vision. The blood moves, so to speak; the mind's eye shifts from focus upon the school girls to the vision of a "Ledaean body, bent / Above a sinking fire." The vision produces a frenzy in the poet's soul: "thereupon my heart is driven wild: / She stands before me as a living child." From there, the vision proceeds, casting Maud Gonne in her present image, the antithesis of the child-image. This draws to the poet's mind his own image: "I though never of Ledaean kind / Had pretty plumage once." Recollection of his animal beauty ("plumage") begins for the poet a reverie, a double consciousness, capable of seeing past, present and future simultaneously. When Yeats writes that it is "better to smile on all that smile, and show / There is a comfortable kind of old scarecrow," he transforms self. Uncomfortable in one instance with the children, the church, his own mutability, he becomes comfortable because of the transformation through memory.

However, the poet moves beyond becoming just comfortable with his passions. He ultimately moves into sublime experience. "What youthful mother," Yeats writes,

> Would think her son, did she but see that shape
> With sixty or more winters on its head,
> A compensation for the pang of his birth,
> Or the uncertainty of his setting forth?

Likely, the mother would not think the son, in his aged incarnation, a just compensation. As David Young points out, the world, with which the poet forever wrestles, "here converges in the mother and child, victimized by the 'honey of generation' and trapped, like the artist, in the problem of reconciling the real and the ideal" (91). This convergence is the significance of the images Yeats saw. "Both nuns and mothers worship images" that "break hearts," regardless the form in which those images are cast. As Ellmann says, "Only images escape the disintegration of age" (*Yeats* 252). Recognizing the unaging aspect of the image forces Yeats to aesthetic action. Thus, comes the invocation:

O Presences
That passion, piety or affection knows,
And that all heavenly glory symbolise—
O self-born mockers of man's enterprise, . . .

This seems a prophetic word, coupled as it is with the following intense revelation[12]:

Labor is blossoming or dancing where
The body is not bruised to pleasure soul,
Nor beauty born out of its own despair,
Nor blear-eyed wisdom out of midnight oil.
O chestnut tree, great rooted blossomer,
Are you the leaf, the blossom or the bole?
O body swayed to music, O brightening glance,
How can we know the dancer from the dance?

Here, then, is the retrieval of pleasurable passion in the vision that sees things simultaneously. Yeats moves through the gamut of passionate emotions: from despair to contentment, and then to ecstasy. He illustrates how we worship images that may break our hearts; if we worship our bodies, for example, we may agonize over their decrepitude. Ellmann discusses it as follows: "For in life the body is bruised to pleasure soul, beauty comes only from despair at its lack, and wisdom is tainted by the toil with which it is gained" (*Identity* 230). The image is always one of many "Presences" known to passion, to piety, and to affection. Precisely, the image is "the dancer and the dance" simultaneously—not just the "chestnut tree," but "the leaf, the blossom," and "the bole." As the anima bruta metaphor suggests, humanity is not just a contemplative, emotional creature, but a passionate beast. Ultimately, this knowledge is a matter of extreme ecstasy and wisdom. Ecstasy makes it possible not to bruise the body despite its decrepitude, for we are able to look beyond the shallow joy of the merely physical to the joy found in the Unity of Being.[13]

Probably no other single poem illustrates the anima bruta metaphor as well as "Leda and the Swan." In "Among School Children," past and present images merge together, creating a sort of procreative dance, blossoming coming out of the aged body. Together, "Among School Children" and "Leda and the Swan" are emblematic of Yeats's concentric cones; they illustrate the opposing spirings of the universe, the one procreative and the other destructive. In "Leda and the Swan," the poet entertains how present action merges with future, creating destruction.[14] Uncontrolled passion may produce destructive tendencies; it may be brutish. Thus, in "Leda and the Swan" the passionate entity takes the shape of the swan, by now a recognized symbol in Yeats's poetry. Bernard Levine points out a curious contrast between Leda and her antagonist, the Swan. He notes

> the reflexive opposition of concrete and abstract imagery. Leda, 'the staggering girl,' is identified through concrete detail: 'Her thighs,' 'her nape,' 'her helpless breast,' 'her loosening thighs.' The swan, on the other hand, is never referred to in the poem itself as a 'swan.' He is described as an overpowering abstraction—'the great wings,' 'the dark webs,' 'that white rush,' 'the brute blood,' 'the indifferent beak.' (114-15)

This is certainly interesting on a rhetorical level, but it is also worth noting on a metaphorical one. Leda, metaphorically, is equal to all humanity. That she is described in concrete terms attests to her indisputable place among humankind. She is at once victim of and privy to something miraculous. God has shown her favor, though the consummation of the favor is an act of violent and sensuous passion. Can the two happen concurrently? Yeats must think so, for look how he uses the vocabulary of sexuality. "A sudden blow" is the attack, but "the great wings beating still" makes the attack ambiguous. The wings still beat, or they are beating into quietness. I think the preferable reading is the latter, for Yeats continues the juxtaposition of the violent against the sensuous in the very next line, in the very same pattern. The girl is "staggering," but her thighs are "caressed." In the third line, the order is reversed. "Dark webs" suggest more than just the swan's feet; they suggest the mysterious web of passion. This is juxtaposed against the more violent "her nape caught in his bill." This alternation of violent rhetoric juxtaposed to sensual rhetoric repeats itself numerous times throughout the poem.

Consider the ambiguous second stanza; the pattern mentioned above is maintained, but the added interrogative function of the sentences prompts further examination into the nature of passion. Yeats writes,

> How can those terrified vague fingers push
> The feathered glory from her loosening thighs?
> And how can body, laid in that white rush,
> But feel the strange heart beating where it lies?

How, indeed? Forget the juxtapositions for the time being and consider what the questions suggest. In the first instance, the reader might suppose Yeats wonders how Leda can ever hope to push the beast away; she is, after all, "terrified" and over-powered. However, Yeats defuses this interpretation by his employment of other key words. Those fingers are not just "terrified," they are also "vague." The fingers do not know what they are supposed to do because of the "glory" of her seducer, or because she has no "knowledge" of what is happening. Even "her loosening thighs" suggest the ambiguity of her body's response. Perhaps Leda submits, and it may seem almost a surrender when Yeats makes use of words such as "vague" and "loosening." Thus, the line seems more appropriately interpreted as "how could she ever want to push the swan from her?" The second question illustrates, essentially, the mingling of the lovers' spirits. The sex act is a "white rush" of emotions; their hearts drum against each other.[15]

Despite the original violence of the strange coupling, something transpires during the throes of passion that make Leda one with her attacker. Yeats's use of the metaphor says something essential about "the brute blood of the air." Levine missed it, though he came close to the idea when he puzzled over the mixture of the concrete and the abstract. Passion is both concrete and abstract, it is both human and godly, it is both sensuous and violent, and it is both vulnerable and powerful. Just as images coexist in "Among School Children," diverse and antithetical characteristics of passion coexist. Passion certainly is rooted in extremities. The concept reinforces one brought up in the last chapter: the artist's feet must always be rooted in two realms.

This, then, may answer the question posed in the final three lines of "Leda and the Swan":

> So mastered by the brute blood of the air,
> Did she put on his knowledge with his power
> Before the indifferent beak could let her drop?

Many critics have said that it would have been impossible for her to have "put on his knowledge." Bloom, for example, says, "I wish . . . that the Yeats sonnet had just a touch of the Shelleyan skepticism about divine power and knowledge" (364-65). What Bloom fails to realize, perhaps because he cannot see past Shelley's achievement, is that "Leda and the Swan" teems with skepticism on this very point. If it is possible at all that Zeus had knowledge, when you consider the convergence of all other contrary elements in the poem, why should a convergence of the contraries found in "knowledge" and "power" not also take place? Of course, this overlooks the ambiguity of the question. The question leads us to assume that she put on "his power," when in fact she may not have. If she did have "his power," then I would say that she had "his knowledge," too. However, at the risk of sounding contradictory, she may not have had either power or knowledge because the swan, himself, may not have had either.

Richard Ellmann writes a curious thing:

> Power and knowledge, as [Yeats] had said in "Blood and the Moon" and implied in "Leda and the Swan," cannot exist together. Yet there is one escape from mortality: when our eyes are blinded by affection, passion, or piety, like those of a mother, of a lover, or of a nun, we see images which are independent of life or fact. (*Identity* 229)

Ellmann sees the similarity between "Leda and the Swan" and "Among School Children," as I have. But the mention of "Blood and the Moon" requires a close look at yet another poem. The section of "Blood and the Moon" under question is:

> For wisdom is the property of the dead,
> A something incompatibile with life; and power,
> Like everything that has the stain of blood,
> A property of the living; but no stain
> Can come upon the visage of the moon
> When it has looked in glory from a cloud.

Wisdom, or knowledge, then, belongs to the non-living. Power, because it bears "the stain of blood," a passionate characteristic, belongs to the living. But what has this to do with God? God is neither living nor dead; he can manifest himself in either world. If he is non-living, then Wisdom belongs to god; if he lives, Power is his. However, think back to "The Cat and the Moon" where Yeats uses the moon to suggest our God in stasis. In "Blood and the Moon," so long as God "looked in glory from a cloud," "no stain" of power-wrought blood smeared God's face. However, the Swan, which is God, has left his position of glory and come among the living. Therefore, he becomes a creature of blood, just as Leda is a creature of blood. Both have power. The Swan has the power to seduce Leda, and Leda has obviously the power to submit as it seems apparent she chooses to do. But because God is neither living nor non-living, surely he must bear a portion of Wisdom. The passionate act is not necessarily an unthinking act. Rather, the swan chooses to ignore what his omniscience must have revealed would result from his seduction of Leda. He has knowledge, but this is superseded by passion. Then, does Leda have "his power"? Not his, specifically, though she has power. Most of it is hers because she is a creature of blood. She acquires a sense or degree of Zeus's power for she has learned, by immediate act, what may result from aggression or passion. This is gratification.

The powers of passion take her, metaphorically, into the non-living state where Wisdom resides. Yeats writes,

> A shudder in the loins engenders there
> The broken wall, the burning roof and tower
> And Agamemnon dead.
>   Being so caught up,
> So mastered by the brute blood of the air,
> Did she put on his knowledge with his power
> Before the indifferent beak could let her drop?

The word *shudder* may suggest Leda's terror, as too many writers have suggested. However, the word even more dramatically connotes the throes of orgasm; Leda has been "so caught up," she is "mastered by the brute blood of the air." But might it not be as much her "brute blood" as the swan's that controls her? As far as her impregnation goes, the engendering is simultaneously conception and destruction, both living and non-living. Things permeate into negation, a zero, which is perfect, which is whole, which is unity. The part of knowledge Leda puts on, then, is the part Zeus brings with him—the wisdom that chooses to ignore the consequences. Does Zeus regret? No, he is "indifferent." Will Leda regret? No, because she will choose not to.[16] She will give birth to two daughters; rather than see the image of destruction arising from their birth, the mother will, naturally, as Ellmann stated, be "blinded by affection" by the image of the daughters.

However, Ellmann is mistaken when he says that power and knowledge cannot coexist. He further misreads when he sees this as a Yeatsian fact. Time and again Yeats sets up the contraries at extreme poles. Thus, when he writes in "Blood and Moon" about wisdom and power as being properties of the non-living and the living, respectively, he has set up antinomies. The anima bruta metaphor, however, shows conclusively that Yeats wants us to seek after neither this world, specifically, nor the non-living world. Vision takes us to the other world, but it never removes us from this world. Arriving at that spiritual point when we are able to see ourselves astraddle both, able to see images from both simultaneously, is that point of extreme ecstasy when all contraries can coexist. This is where passion is the most intense because the brute impulse of humanity is given the pulse of the spirit of the universe. The mandala, in its elaboration, is nonetheless an unbroken ring. This is the very thing that Fergus understands: with wisdom comes "great webs of sorrow"; but, the added burden of living in ecstasy is to rule "the brazen cars," "the shadow of the wood," "the white breast of the dim sea," and "all dishevelled wandering stars." The world, the universe, is in our control once we have fashioned for ourselves that unbroken ring. The anima bruta metaphor helps get us there.

If we recall "The Indian Upon God," we saw how the creatures of this world portrayed God in their self-image. Though the Indian himself never casts God into his image, one wonders if Yeats has not done so in "Leda and the Swan" metaphorically. He identifies with the swans in "The Wild Swans at Coole." He remarks that he "had pretty plumage once" in "Among School Children," and that his recollection of Maud Gonne establishes her as one of the "Ledaean kind." I do not want to digress with a long discussion upon Yeats's infatuation over Maud Gonne. Rather, I want to assert the possibility that the poem, by virtue of the anima bruta metaphor, is reasonably a metaphorical, psycho-sexual fantasy. If Yeats sees himself as the swan and Maud Gonne as Leda, he is able to use the metaphor to attain sexual gratification from the woman he loved so desperately. The metaphor is a form of sublimation. Furthermore, if Yeats sees himself as a god-figure in the poem, there must exist some obvious transmutation. What has God got that Yeats does not have? Besides the actual sexual gratification, perhaps the will to dominate forcefully; perhaps the ability to indifferently let Maud Gonne drop. More significantly, perhaps most supreme God possesses the control of the artist over the artistic creation. The anima bruta metaphor allows the poet to step into another, malevolent skin to more fully exercise the passions that exist in the meeker body. The metaphor is the ready vehicle for Yeats's Mask; it provides Yeats what Ellmann termed "his policy of concealment of his more intimate self" by "the habiliments of arrogance and power," as "one that ruffled in a manly pose / For all his timid heart" (*Yeats* 171).

Transmutation such as this has its obvious psychological benefits, among them a release of aggression through a non-aggressive channel. In other of Yeats's poems, the anima bruta metaphor allows the poet to create a dialect between the rational self and the animal self. This creates, often, a sort of humorous dialogue that will later shape the "Crazy Jane" poems. In "The Hawk," for example, the rational voice intones,

> 'Call down the hawk from the air;
> Let him be hooded or caged
> Till the yellow eye has grown mild,
> For larder and spit are bare,
> The old cook enraged,
> The scullion gone wild.'

The too-proud bird has not performed its required duties, and the earthbound inhabitants are going hungry. However, the hawk states in no uncertain terms that it "will not be clapped in a hood, / Nor a cage, nor alight upon wrist." It has "learnt to be proud" as it flies "over the wood / in the broken mist / Or tumbling cloud." When the dialogue returns to the voice of rational humanity, we discover the hawk is actually the "yellow-eyed hawk of the mind." The hunger felt by this rational voice is not physical hunger but hunger of another sort. While the bird has soared its imaginative skies, the physical creature has sat "dumbfounded before a knave" and given a friend "a pretense of wit." The physical, rational creature requires the soaring imagination, but cannot summon it at the necessary interval. The separation of imagination from the physical world has a foundering effect. Most often, Yeats seems to lean toward preference of the passionate beast over the more passionless, rational creature. "Dumbfoundedness" is equal to impotency. Anytime such a dialectic occurs, as in "Vacillation" or "A Dialogue of Self and Soul," and numerous other pieces, we find Yeats trying to work out a fusion of the extremities. This differs from "Leda and the Swan," yet the same pattern of creature of the earth struggling, fusing, converging with creature of the air takes place here. This is, generally, a fundamental pattern in the anima bruta metaphor.

Yeats adheres to this pattern in "His Phoenix." In the first four lines of the poem Yeats deliberately alludes to "Leda and the Swan." A "queen in China, or maybe it's in Spain," has such beauty "a whiteness with no stain, / That she might be that sprightly girl trodden by a bird." Of course, this queen is not Leda. If we read the heavy metrical beat on the word *might*, we understand immediately the implausibility of this. As well, Yeats does not say *swan* but *bird*. Thus, while he draws the allusion, he is also very careful about defusing the very thing he has just asserted. One has to wonder why Yeats does this. Likely, it is to show firmly that even a most beautiful queen as this cannot equal the beauty of the Ledaean body—not just the one in mythology but emphatically the one Yeats says "I knew." An entire catalogue of beautiful women, "the breakers of men's hearts" and the "engines of delight," occupy this poem. However, none of these women are visions of undying beauty. Yeats says, "I knew a phoenix in my youth, so let them have their day." How Maud Gonne is a phoenix was illustrated in "Among School Children." The vision of the woman keeps arising in the flames of the passionate man's mind.

Vision is clearly one of the results of the anima bruta metaphor. In every example I have discussed thus far in this chapter, *vision* has played a principal role. Even as Yeats experimented with the visionary in the earlier poems, he had discovered the aesthetic freedoms a double consciousness gave him. He specifically addresses this visionary phenomena and its relationship to the anima bruta metaphor in "The Double Vision of Michael Robartes." The persona of the poem immediately asserts the awareness of the two spheres he occupies. Yeats writes,

> the mind's eye
> Has called up the cold spirits that are born
> When the old moon is vanished from the sky
> And the new still hides her horn.

We are stuck between phases, here; we are neither under the influence of the old or new moon.[17] When Yeats writes "Under blank eyes and fingers never still / The particular is pounded till it is man," he refers to both the Adamic creation as well as God's manipulation of the human species. For under the old moon's influence, the persona wonders, "When had I my own will? / O not since life began." Furthermore, under this moon's influence, humanity is

> Constrained, arraigned, baffled, bent and unbent
> By these wire-jointed jaws and limbs of wood,
> Themselves obedient,
> Knowing not evil and good;
> Obedient to some hidden magical breath.
> They do not even feel, so abstract are they,
> So dead beyond our death,
> Triumph that we obey.

The tonal and metrical qualities of these lines create metaphor, too. First, the sound of the words *constrained*, *arraigned*, *baffled*, *bent*, *unbent* suggests the very action they denote; the sound manipulates the lines, constraining the language in a barrage of consonantal and assonantal shifts. Interestingly, *constrained* and *arraigned* rhyme, as do *bent* and *unbent.* However, the form of the words alter from an initial consonant to an initial vowel. The word *baffled* is poised between the rhyming though shifting words, as if *baffled* occupies the confused position. Even the meter of this particular line suggests the action:

> ˘ ´ ˘ ´ ´ ˘ ´ ˘ ˘ ´
> Constrained, | arraigned, | baffled, | bent and | unbent

The first two feet are iambic; the second two feet, beginning with the *baffled* word, are trochaic; the fifth foot returns, in "unbent" fashion, to the iambic pattern. The lines become puppets controlled by the master puppeteer, the poet. Meanwhile, puppetted humanity, "dead beyond our death," has no will of its own nor control over its own destiny because of the influence of the old moon. Yet, when Michael Robartes finds himself between phases he has the "Chance and Choice" of his double vision.

While accutely aware of the lifelessness of physical life, the vision shows

Robartes the liveliness of the visionary world. Whereas passions do not exist under the constraints of the moon, passions thrive in the visionary world. In the vision, he "suddenly saw / A Sphinx with woman breast and lion paw," and "a Buddha, hand at rest, / Hand lifted up that blest." The Sphinx and lion image will come up in a subsequent poem, "The Second Coming," and the reference to Buddha ties this poem to Yeats's interest in Eastern mysticism. When Yeats tries so often to bring to his poems the configuration of the mandala, of Unity of Being, Buddha occupies a hallowed, though not necessarily holy, position in this poem.

Because of these presences, the vision assumes sacredness. The "hand lifted up that blest" blesses not only what transpires in the vision but also the visionary man, giving him passage into the visionary world. The vision is concrete; Michael Robartes says, "I saw it all in the mind's eye / There can be nothing solider till I die." Even when the vision vanishes, reality will not be as concrete as the vision. The vision supersedes reality; it takes predominance over the persona's spirit. What Robartes sees is:

> right between these two a girl at play
> That, it may be, had danced her life away,
> For now being dead it seemed
> That she of dancing dreamed.

The placement of the girl between the Sphinx and Buddha is important. Not only is Robartes between the phases of the old moon and the new, stuck between the rational and the passionate, the girl is stuck between two entities possessing antithetical qualities. Metaphorically, the old moon is the Sphinx and the new moon is Buddha; metaphorically, Robartes and the dancer are of a kind. This is defended simply by studying two of the stanzas closely. In the first of these, the Sphinx

> lashed her tail; her eyes lit by the moon
> Gazed upon all things known, all things unknown,
> In triumph of intellect
> With motionless head erect.

The all-knowing, unchanging intelligence is juxtaposed by Buddha:

> That other's moonlit eyeballs never moved,
> Being fixed on all things loved, all things unloved,
> Yet little peace he had,
> For those that love are sad.

Buddha has nothing to do with knowledge, for his interest is fixed upon the extremities of love. He is the antithesis of the Sphinx. The girl, meanwhile, holds center position; her dancing forms its own circle of existence:

> O little did they care who danced between,
> And little she by whom her dance was seen
> So she had outdanced thought.
> Body perfection brought, . . .

The dance elevates her beyond thought and her body brings her perfection beyond Buddha's. Robartes identifies with this image, and this identification moves him beyond thought and bodily (or passionate) perfection. He says, "I knew that I had seen, had seen at last / That girl my unremembering nights hold fast," and that the newly attained, re-attained dream flings "into my meat / A crazy juice that makes the pulses beat." "Being caught between the pull / Of the dark moon and the full" by the vision of the dancer, Michael Robartes undergoes what Martin calls "art's reconciliation of body and mind" (69). This reconcilement strikes an eternal balance. However, note that this balance is not dichotimized in the individual. Everything is swirled together in the motion of the dancer. Yeats clarifies what he means in "Michael Robartes and the Dancer" when the persona says, "That blest souls are not composite."[18]

A transformation must take place, then, if blessèdness is to occur. Some sort of dancing must take place, some acute action that carries the "dancer" into euphoria. However, Yeats does not let us reside in the blessèd state for long. As always, he goes on to illustrate an alternative situation, testing his instincts and passions, scrutinizing his hypotheses and metaphors for their consistency. One such alternative situation is found in "Easter 1916." This poem immortalizes the rebels who possessed a dream and loved Ireland so much it moved them to violence. Before their transformation into rebels, they seem very much a part of the common herd: "That woman's days were spent / In ignorant good-will, / Her nights in argument"; "This man had kept a school"; "This other his helper and friend / Was coming into his force"; "This other man . . . / A drunken, vainglorious lout." Each of these characters, Yeats says, has "resigned" parts "in the casual comedy." They have given up the comedic, normal existence. Passion over politics turns them into rebels; as Yeats puts it,

> Hearts with one purpose alone
> Through summer and winter seem
> Enchanted to a stone
> To trouble the living stream.

This is what Yeats means when he says these people have been "transformed utterly: / A terrible beauty is born." Their transformation moves them from one extremity to another. Transformation is necessary if we are to come to blessèdness, but to transform *utterly* is to vacillate too far toward the other extreme. Transformation is beautiful, but this type makes it a "terrible beauty."

Carmel Jordan writes that

> by the third stanza . . . all words and movements have been replaced by the hard cold image of the stone—"The stone's in the midst of all"—which dominates the poem from that point on. Yeats mentions the stone three times in the last two stanzas and then immediately recites the names of the executed rebels who, through the Mask of death, have moved "beyond the visible world" and assumed the cold final beauty of stone themselves. (76)

While I agree in part with Jordan's premise, that the stone becomes the central image throughout the remainder of the poem, "cold final beauty" does not equal the starkness of Yeats's antithetical "terrible beauty." Recall, if you would, my discussion of "The Cat and the Moon." The moon troubles the cat's animal blood, just as the stone-metaphor troubles "the living stream" in this poem. The "living stream" is the blood-stream; the stone, the unwavering principles of the fanatic heart, is as locked up in orbit as the cat's moon. Yeats writes that "too long a sacrifice / Can make a stone of the heart." He asks, "O when may it suffice?" The answer to the question is

> Heaven's part, our part
> To murmur name upon name,
> As a mother names her child
> When sleep at last has come
> On limbs that had run wild.

The naming of names brings the dead to life again, making them more heroic in the image than they were, perhaps, in real life. Although "Easter 1916" predates "Among School Children," the power of the image to transcend life and death is evident here. Yeats asks whether it was "needless death after all," when clearly the evocative image says it was not. It is "enough / To know they dreamed and are dead." The "terrible beauty," however, is that loss of convergence with all extremities; "excess of love / Bewildered them till they died." The rebels are complete in extremity, but not in Unity of Being.

However, the poet is able to find himself in Unity of Being by being both part of the "living stream" and part of the "stone." When the poet creates these paradoxes, he wants to place himself between the phases of the moon, caught up in the dance. As Thomas Whitaker says,

> For him the present is nonexistent except as a locus of reverie over the tapestries of past and future. But Yeats came to see that the trump of judgment must blow now, that the world must end in every poem. Like Nietzsche's suprahistorical man, the speaker must be one for whom "the world is complete and fulfills its aim in every single moment." Such a man is most fully in time even as he most fully transcends it. Hence transcience and transcendence begin to fuse . . . . (273)

Perhaps this fusion is best exemplified by "The Second Coming." Past and present merge and shape the future. We have seen how closely aligned birds are to the blood nature of humanity in Yeats's poetry; although, as Northrup Frye notes, "the bird is often the swan, for obvious reasons," "The Second Coming" incorporates species from his "parliament of fowls" (21).

The opening stanza not only calls to mind the lighter dilemma of "The Hawk," it conjures the political upheavals of Ireland, as exemplified in "Easter 1916." Yeats's anima bruta metaphor creates a sort of cohesiveness that is unmistakable—it is a blood wash that marks indelibly most of his poems. Most readers know "The Second Coming" very well, yet I think the opening stanza bears requoting:

> Turning and turning in the widening gyre
> The falcon cannot hear the falconer;
> Things fall apart; the centre cannot hold;
> Mere anarchy is loosed upon the world,
> The blood-dimmed tide is loosed, and everywhere
> The ceremony of innocence is drowned;
> The best lack all conviction, while the worst
> Are full of passionate intensity.

Structurally, the opening stanza is very interesting. Just as that falcon gets farther and farther away from its master, the center of the universe gets farther and farther away from its controlling origin. Innocence cannot survive long before it is drowned by the tide of corruption; and the best and the worst pursue interests antithetical to their characters.

Compare the structure of this opening stanza to this portion of the second:

> somewhere in sands of the desert
> A shape with lion body and the head of a man,

A gaze blank and pitiless as the sun,
Is moving its slow thighs, while all about it
Reel shadows of the indignant desert birds.
The darkness drops again; but now I know
That twenty centuries of stony sleep
Were vexed to nightmare by a rocking cradle,
And what rough beast, its hour come round at last,
Slouches towards Bethlehem to be born?

Where the first stanza suggests all things unwinding, the spring broken, the second stanza is its direct metaphorical opposite. This stanza tightens. The "turning and turning" and "widening" of the first stanza illustrate the unravelling of the universe; however, the diction of the second stanza is a reeling in of the universe. Rather than things being "loosed," as they are in the first stanza, things are drawn into the "moving . . . slow thighs" of the beast. The "indignant desert birds" "reel." The falcons spin outward, but the word reel suggests an inward draw. Literally, this is correct. The desert birds *reel* in circles until their carrion is found; they circle in upon it, drawing themselves closer to the earth, pulling their circle closer and tighter, until finally they have claimed their prize. Even the "rough beast" comes "round." Thus, if the first stanza equals the anarchy of the world, the second stanza equals the tyrannical control of the forthcoming, envisioned world. The pattern and the world are completely inverted between the two stanzas.

The importance of this inversion to the anima bruta metaphor is its imaginative link between the real world and the idealized world, the physical world and the non-physical world, the world of unrelenting intellect and the world of boundless passion. All these worlds exist simultaneously, intertwined in that orgiastic mandala—providing, of course, we possess vision of the blessèd state. What Yeats sees, however, is the world that has lost vision. The trouble of the world is its penchant for becoming "enchanted to a stone," of becoming too much the old, unchangable moon. This trouble troubles "the living stream," "the animal blood."[19] As A. G. Stock says, Yeats is "intensely aware of man in history and of the soul in eternity"; at times he sees "history as an image of the soul writ large"; he sees "an uncongenial world disintegrating and an unknowable future taking shape in the surrounding dark" (188).

Part of the awareness that Stock notes is founded in orthodox, western religion. A. Norman Jeffares explains, "[W]e realize that in the Yeatsian system modern civilization had its initial impulse in the teachings of Christ. He may, in this poem, be the falconer who began an era of history which has almost reached its conclusion . . ." (109). If the falconer is Christ, then the falcon is humanity. Yeats uses the metaphor for Christianity to create an alternative metaphor to supersede it. Jeffares calls this succession a revolution, "a catastrophic change 'from circle to point,' the point being the apex of an historical period beginning its course in an opposite direction" (109). Metaphor, then, replaces metaphor. By extension, Christianity is a metaphor for a system of beliefs. Yeats illustrates it as a metaphor that seeks to control our animal impulses, limiting the opportunity of Choice and Chance. If the metaphor has lost both function and purpose, an antithetical metaphor might replace it.

Bloom doubts strongly Jeffares's interpretation. He says,

> It seems likelier that the falconer, rather than the falcon, represents man, and the falcon his mastery of nature, now in the act of falling apart. The center is man; he cannot hold the falcon to an imposed discipline, and the widening gyre is therefore one with the loosing of anarchy upon the world. (321)

Bloom's reading is intriguing for a few reasons. First, the falconer's inability to control the falcon seems a natural occurrence once humanity becomes too removed from nature; the "humane" ideals create the separation. Second, and Bloom fails to make the point, the falconer's failure to control the falcon is emblematic of his failure to control his own brutishness. The one is symptomatic of the other. Importantly, though, where Bloom attempts to render Jeffares's interpretation invalid, I think Bloom has actually, and unwittingly, validated Jeffares's position. After all, Christ was a man, he was human. Supposed holiness notwithstanding, the emblem of spiritual perfection was flesh, and he was the center of the western world, and subsequent Christianity has been the "imposed discipline" of human nature.

Interestingly, the Christian metaphor is not a bloodless one, just as Yeats's metaphors are not. The Christian premise is built upon the notion of sacrifice and atonement through blood. Thus, a metaphor of blood itself, it has had its rebellious day, but turned to stone. The animal blood in the falcon cannot hear the falconer any longer because the falconer has lost touch with his own animal blood. Out of control, animal passions produce a "blood-dimmed tide." The blood metaphor attributed to the falconer becomes a bloodless one, one in which life's breath has ceased. We might assume the metaphor that replaces it will be a blood metaphor, too. Not exactly, however. The "shape with lion body and the head of a man, / A gaze blank and pitiless as the sun" is equivalent to the Sphinx we saw in "The Double Vision of Michael Robartes."[20] Therefore, the creature at this point is all reason, pitiless and unrelenting. It is not a blood creature at all. This may account for why the desert birds are "indignant." Blood creatures, just like the falcon, just like humanity, they are troubled by the non-blood creature. Still the desert birds reel down, for the "rough beast" is slouching toward Bethlehem. I make much of the word *rough*. The beast's unrelenting dispensation of authority makes it rough, or powerful. But *rough beast* also suggests *unfinished* beast. What the desert birds know instinctively is what transpires as the beast moves from its "stony sleep" toward Bethlehem: he becomes a creature of blood at the end of his metaphorical phase.

The beast is not born until its reign is complete, until its slouching is done. As Donald Davie notes, "The meaning of the poem is in the calculated collision in the last line of the words 'slouches' and 'Bethlehem'" (79). Furthermore, "What the poem says is that when the superhuman invades the human realm all that the human can say of it is that it is non-human: there can be no discriminating at such a time between subhuman and superhuman, between bestial and divine" (79). Thus, as occurred in "Leda and the Swan," a convergence of the human and the spiritual takes place, and this convergence leads us, if temporarily, into a sort of perfected state of unity. The outbound world rebounds upon itself and unity is reestablished. The anima bruta metaphor illustrates how the too rational creature is ever needful of the blessèdness that blood gives the creature; the too passionate creature is ever needful of a good portion of reason. But the composite creature is not blessèd; blessèdness comes from the resolution of all extremities: the turning, the reeling, the rocking of those who dance the dance of the universe.

CHAPTER 4

ADAM'S CURSE: YEATS'S METAPOETICS

The diversity of metaphorical designs in Yeats's poetry confirms his principle that no poet "can do the same thing twice if he has put much mind into it" (*Explorations* 430). We examined a variety of metaphorical techniques in Chapter 1; the conceptual metaphor of the island wanderer in Chapter 2 illustrated several aesthetic principles; and, the anima bruta metaphor in Chapter 3 verified the reconciliatory laws of humanity's duality. Granted, the metaphorical pattern may be repeated, but its actual employment in any poem reveals an innovative resolution to what seems the poet's familiar "quarrel" with self (*Mythologies* 331). Yeats's constant repetition of the metaphorical concepts, and his endless refinement and testings of his metaphors is further complicated by the interrelationship of the variable repetitions. Yeats's metaphorical patterns often impose their characteristics upon poems that seem, upon first reading, to belong categorically to another pattern. This overlapping quality or fusion suggests that repetition and fusion join in yet another concept, another metaphor for poetry which Yeats has rooted self-consciously in art. As Andrew Parkin says, because of "Yeats's dramatic imagination," "on the whole in Yeats's poetry, . . . things do not fall apart, and mere anarchy is not loosed upon his readers" (49). The poems that illustrate aesthetic consciousness and employ a set of art-related nerves become products of a metaphor for art. Specifically, in Yeats's verse the poem as art-form is often a self-defining treatise upon art's methodology. As Yeats describes it in "The Statues," "mirror on mirror mirrored is all the show." In other words, the poem tells us what art is, and because of this definition we understand more about the nature of poetry.

From the early poems to the late ones, from "The Song of the Happy

Shepherd's" "words alone are certain good" to the "artifice of eternity" in the Byzantium poems, art's methodology, its techniques, and its purposes occupy Yeats's mind. Art leads Yeats ever closer to his concept of Unity of Being, of a wholeness not only in the art itself but in the heart and soul of the poet. In his *Autobiography*, Yeats writes how he

> had been put into a rage by the followers of Huxley, Tyndall, Carolus Duran, and Bastien-Lepage, who not only asserted the unimportance of subject whether in art or literature, but the independence of the arts from one another. Upon the other hand, I delighted in every age where poet and artist confined themselves gladly to some inherited subject-matter known to the whole people, for I thought that in man and race alike there is something called "Unity of Being," using that term as Dante used it when he compared beauty in the *Convito* to a perfectly proportioned human body. (*Autobiography* 128)

The "inherited subject-matter" occupies Yeats's poetry. He salvages subject and emblem from Irish folklore, instance and longing recalled from his own life, and symbol and image from the cultural consciousness of the anima mundi, and incorporates these elements into his work. The "inherited subject matter" carries with it the inheritance of concerns for craft as a subject, too. This, then, creates an art-conscious art.

As seer, the poet senses art's significance to self and its prophetic worth to the sense-less "common herd of humanity." The metaphoric message is clear enough for those who read "The Song of the Happy Shepherd" for the aesthetic metaphor: art breathes new life into the diseased world, it replaces Time's cracked tune with syncopation, and it emphasizes that words, only, are valuable because they help us to live and to dream. The poem suggests we ought to trust language, to have faith in it, and it implies the necessity of our using language to generate our happiness. What is art, then? No less than perfected God, it would seem. Humanity's creation and self-creation, art is the spiritual center of our existence.

In "Adam's Curse," Yeats provides us with many significant points about aesthetics. The poem is self-consciously about poetry, though the "inherited subject-matter" is the Adamic myth. Art, then, is metaphorically Adam's curse, and it is also the curse all of us bear. John Unterecker notes the poem's "discussion of three parallel labors: the poet's, the beautiful woman's, and the lover's" (99), but the poem is about more than these labors. First, labor is the burden of all humanity. Barton Friedman says the poem "sums up the curse Adam has visited upon the world; for labor—as the pangs of childbirth, the stitching and unstitching of the poet's line, the preparation of a woman's face

—comprises man's struggle against the erosive effects of time" (112-13). Labor, then, is humanity's guarantee of perpetual existence. We must work to survive. If art is labor (and Yeats says in "Adam's Curse" art is "to work harder" than any other labor), it must also guarantee our survival. The metaphorical equivalence makes this an implicit truth.

However, both Friedman and Unterecker miss an important point about the similarities between Adam's curse and art. Granted, art is hard work; like the woman who works at her own physical beauty, the poet must work at art to make it beautiful. However, part of Adam's curse was expulsion from Edenic paradise; part of it was death. These notions are implied by the poem's title, and the loss of Paradise may be noted at the poem's conclusion. "I strove / To love you in the old high way of love" suggests a specific loss of Paradise, the one founded upon romantic love. However, in many other poems Yeats specifically addresses the dilemma of securing the lost paradisaical world. In part, this is what "The Lake Isle of Innisfree" and "Sailing to Byzantium" illustrate. While the poet never secures Paradise in the physical, art at least is the means by which it may be retrieved imaginatively. The curse, then, is Paradise's intangibility; we can have Paradise, but only through art. Art as curse is how it reminds us of the imperfect world in which we reside. Like God, art taunts us with heaven while it frustrates us with the hell of our world.

Next, if art is death, we must wonder how this is so. Yeats does not account for this equivalence in "Adam's Curse." However, I think this notion is obvious enough in other poems. As in the anima bruta metaphor, where the moment of orgasm is simultaneous death and life, the aesthetic metaphor suggests a similar pattern in the creative act of writing. Crazy Jane says that "nothing can be sole or whole / That has not been rent" ("Crazy Jane Talks with the Bishop"); this may be a description of the procreative process, but it might just as well be a description of the creative process of writing. In Yeats's case, a poem may draw him nearer to his own mutability, his own decrepitude, his own death, "when all is ruin once again" ("To Be Carved on a Stone at Thoor Ballylee"). Yet, the poem may simultaneously draw him to where "men dance on deathless feet" ("Mohini Chatterjee"). Without art, life certainly is death; humanity becomes "the noisy set" "the martyrs call the world." Finding nothing of any particular value, humanity is content to live an empty, deathly life, unlike the "martyrs"—or poets—who are willing to die through the creative act to enhance life. The poet "has found no comfort in the grave" ("The Man Who Dreamed of Faeryland"), though the grave may lead the poet to a comforting understanding of human existence.

What have we learned thus far, then, from the self-reflexivity of poetry? One, as seen in "The Song of the Happy Shepherd," that words heal, that they are good, that they can make us happy. Two, as seen in "Adam's Curse," that art is labor, that art is the curse of expulsion from Paradise and the effort to retrieve it; that, implicitly, art is "the carrier of death" (Derrida 17) while it is simultaneously the protector against it. Still, art is more than just these concepts. In "Among School Children," Yeats wrote, "Labour is blossoming or dancing where / The body is not bruised to pleasure soul." If art is labor, as "Adam's Curse" suggests, then "[Art] is blossoming or dancing," too. The self-reflexivity of Yeats's verses often illustrate the concept of poetry as dance and dancer (for "How can we know the dancer from the dance?").

As a metaphor for art, dancer and dance signify the other-worldliness of the artist and the artist's creation; it illustrates how artist and art are ecstatically entwined. As I discussed in Chapter 3, the motion of dance is connected to the "brute blood" of humanity; the form of the dance, a "fine thing" ("Adam's Curse"), is connected to anima. Frank Kermode says that "proportion, movement, meaning, are not intellectual properties, but belong to that reality of the imagination which is a symbolic reality. The beauty of a woman, and particularly of a woman in movement, is the emblem of the work of art or Image" (57). Furthermore, Kermode says the "dancer . . . reconciles antithetical movements: the division of soul and body, form and matter, life and death, artist and audience" (60). When the polarities are reconciled, unity ensues. As Frances Oppel says,

> True art reconnects humans with their source, which in a mystical sense is both beginning and end, both 'first-moved' and 'the flame of the Last Day.' Blake calls the source God, and Yeats follows.
> True art as defined by Yeats-Blake seeks the fulfillment of desire, the reuniting of love and death. False art is an instrument, not of death (which, as the dialectical counterpart of Eros, is part of 'life'), but of 'evil'—repression, desexualization, the deadened life, or the 'modern' way of materialism, moderation, and morality as Yeats defines the 'opponent' in "The Literary Movement in Ireland." (37)

The "fulfillment of desire, the reuniting of love and death" is an important Yeatsian point. In the "stitching and unstitching" ("Adam's Curse") of a poem, Yeats reconciles the antithetical universe. These words suggest motion, and it is a motion to which the artist gives form. He loses himself in the dance which his poetry becomes. *Dance* is an essential term. The poet's imagination is entwined with the poet's world; in dance's whirling, contraries are not so much mediated as they are dissolved. The dance's fire consumes body, mind, and spirit. As Ellmann says, "The fires of the imagination have a characteristic which distinguishes them from the fires of this world: they burn and do not burn. They are all-powerful to purge images of any experimental dross, but impotent to singe a sleeve" (*Identity* 222). These fires are the passionate fires of creativity; they equal the passions of creative dance.

Consider the short poem, "Sweet Dancer." The girl's dance is emblematic of the dance of our antithetical existences. She "goes dancing there / On the leaf-sown, new-mown, smooth / Grass plot of the garden." She seems to be the same dancer of "The Double Vision of Michael Robartes," moved from the visionary world to what seems the more temporal, physical world. Notice where her dance occurs: in the art-retrieved Paradise of the garden. However, Yeats writes that she has "escaped from her bitter youth, / Escaped out of her crowd." No longer part of constraining past nor part of the rest of humanity, the artist is a creature alone in the motions of her own creation. Furthermore, like the hawk in "The Hawk," she has come "out of her black cloud." Metaphorically, she has not been called to earth by some master's voice; rather, she has come to earth, other-world passions still intact, to dance her dance because, simply, such is the artistic impulse. The "strange men" mentioned in the poem belong to the "noisy set" Yeats mentioned in "Adam's Curse." Because her art takes her from accepted normalcy, she risks martyrdom. She risks being led away because "she is happy being crazy." However, what she does is so beautiful and enchanting, the persona of the poem pleads that she be allowed to "finish her dance." Edward Engelberg says,

> As a leit-motiv, the human form acts as a kind of "rhythm of metaphor"; Yeats himself admitted the Noh dramatists seemed less interested in the human form than "in the rhythm to which it moves, and the triumph of [the dancer's] . . . art is to express the rhythm in its intensity." . . . In essence, like the danse macabre, the dance in Yeats synthesizes an allegory: the pulse of life and the stillness of death stop time with the momentary hesitation of great intensity. (141)

The dancer in "Sweet Dancer" manifests that intensity thoroughly. In her is the "pulse of life." The cessation of dance would be metaphorically equivalent to the cessation of life. Take the artist away, and you take away the art. Conversely, take away the need to express art and you murder the artist. The two are inseparable; the only way to "finish" the dance is to finish living. Also of importance is the obvious presence of audience. The persona wants the dance to continue because the liveliness of the dance breathes life into the viewer. The persona's joy is contrasted by the "strange men's" lack of understanding. But the imaginative mind—at least Yeats's imaginative mind—sees the dance as something already in motion and perpetual. That imagination sees the dance's eternal and spiritual significance. Therefore, if art is dance, then art is also eternal and spiritually significant.

Thus far I have already discussed many concepts about what poetry says art is. However, many of Yeats's poems deal with art as subject even more self-consciously than these examples. An example of such a poem is "The Grey Rock," for here the poet narrates a story concerned with not only story but also with techniques of story-telling. Post-modern fiction writers would call this metafiction, though here, because this is a narrative poem, we might make the signification *metapoetry*. The poet begins the piece, telling us,

> Here's an old story I've re-made,
> Imagining 'twould better please
> Your ears than stories now in fashion,
> Though you may think I waste my breath
> Pretending that there can be passion
> That has more life in it than death, . . .

Already Yeats juxtaposes the contraries of two worlds, one old and the other new, and that passion has life and death in it. Emphasis is placed upon the word *pretending*, for apparently the persona's audience believes death has a greater portion of passion than life does. However, the persona's tale is not a story "now in fashion"; thus, it illustrates how passion attends life, and how art can breathe life into us if we but choose to learn from its examples.

As the persona stages the story, he reiterates that this is a story about a story: "When cups went round at close of day— / Is not that how good stories run?" Specifically, the gods have joined in "drowsy song, or snored," and drank the "juice that made them wise." The juice, in turn, brings before "the dim / Imaginations of their eyes" a vision of a woman "trembling with her passion." As metapoetry, Yeats intersects the unnatural world with the natural world. The drowsy gods are equal to the persona's audience; the persona and his story are equal to the woman and her story. If the persona wants to bring life to his audience, we might assume the woman hopes for lively passion *among* or passionate results *from* the gods. The persona's ability to see these parallels equals aesthetic vision. The vision intrudes upon whatever reveries are taking place, in the tavern or in the presence of gods; the vision demands notice. The story-teller says, "We should be dazed and terror-struck, / If we but saw in dreams that room" of the gods. Metapoetically, however, despite the obviousness of the woman's tale and the persona's tale, we must remember Yeats is telling us both and that somehow we have become his audience. Are we as drowsy as the gods, as drunken as the persona's friends? Is it the persona or Yeats speaking in the following?:

> Since, tavern comrades, you have died,

Maybe your images have stood,
Mere bone and muscle thrown aside,
Before that roomful or as good.

This quatrain poses a curious ambiguity. The story-teller or Yeats (it is impossible at this point to know which is which since Yeats's metapoetics have entwined all levels of interpretation) addresses his "tavern comrades," but says, "you have died." He imagines their "images" before a roomful of gods, just as the woman stands before hers. Does Yeats mean that the persona's current companions are dead, does he mean his own companions of past times, or does he mean our own lifeless presence before our gods, before our select crowd?[1] Since mortal and immortal realms are continually entwined in Yeats, I imagine he means all possibilities. The parallels between the woman, the persona, and the poet, and between the gods, the tavern crowd, and us are essential; as form is an extension of content, three realms—the aesthetic, the natural, and the spiritual—exist superimposed upon each other.

"The Grey Rock" has to do with all the "fine things": love, beauty, heroism, honor, faithfulness. These "things" have to do with art's labors, as noted in "Adam's Curse." Unfortunately, the woman's story illustrates how all those "fine things" have been betrayed, just as the persona's tale suggests how his comrades have betrayed life's passions. Goban, with his "wine adrip," poured it upon the woman and she forgot what had happened and "stared at the gods with laughing lip." The woman's faithfulness is equivalent to the faithfulness of the story-teller, who says at the poem's end, "I have kept my faith, though faith was tried, / To that rock-born, rock-wandering foot, / And the world's altered since you died." Just as the woman is faithful and wants love to survive, so does the story-teller. However, the woman succumbs to drunken forgetfulness; her Lethean sin is equal to the sins of the "bald heads" ("The Scholars"). The persona has not forgot, nor has Yeats; distraught over betrayals of love and all the "fine things," neither enjoy Goban's wine. The persona is in "no good repute" with his "loud host before the sea"; his friends think "sword-strokes were better meant / Than lover's music." In Yeats's case, implicitly, common humanity fails to recognize the vitality of art. All the poet can do is keep writing, hoping that "the wandering foot's content" and that the audience has not fallen asleep.

This poem illustrates, essentially, what Zwerdling notes as "the idea of an actual world intersected at innumerable points by a spiritual one" ("Variations" 86). The catalyst for the crossings must be the aesthetic imagination. This crossing between the artist's physical world and the artist's created world can be seen, also, in the poems "The Magi" and "The Dolls." Consider, first, "The Magi":

Now as at all times I can see in the mind's eye,
In their stiff, painted clothes, the pale unsatisfied ones
Appear and disappear in the blue depth of the sky
With all their ancient faces like rain-beaten stones,
And all their helms of silver hovering side by side,
And all their eyes still fixed, hoping to find once more,
Being by Calvary's turbulence unsatisfied,
The uncontrollable mystery on the bestial floor.

Otto Bohlmann, following Nietzsche's ideas, says this is an example of "history shown as being subject to a rhythm of eternally recurring cycles" (177). However, the Magi in Yeats's poem are a vision and not an historical fact. Nonetheless, Yeats evokes the Christian metaphor, which he reiterates in "The Second Coming," through their image. The image of the Magi resides in the artist's imagination ("Now as at all times I can see in the mind's eye"), as well as in the imaginations of those acquainted with the metaphor. The image is persistent, as persistent as the Magi in their quest. Yeats uses the Magian image, specifically, as an emblem of "recurring cycles," and couples it to the birth-death-resurrection archetype. The wise men are forever the "pale unsatisfied ones" in the poet's mind's eye. Their role in the Christian metaphor, however, is really irrelevant, here; Yeats is not merely making a negative statement about Christianity. In another cycle, another time, the Magi would be for Yeats just as "unsatisfied." The wise men "appear and disappear in the blue depth of the sky," just as our individual thoughts appear and disappear in the recesses of our unconscious and conscious minds. The wise men pursue whatever truth of existence they might find, as if truth were illustrated as "Calvary's turbulence." They will forever remain "unsatisfied," forever seek the "uncontrollable mystery" of eternity, much the way a poet forever seeks out his or her poetic material.

When critics limit themselves to the single mythological reading, they fail to notice that "The Magi" is more a metaphor for art than it is historicism or mythological criticism. The artistic mind seeks a metaphor of art that defines Unity of Being. Such a metaphor may derive from mythological roots, but the metaphor transcends the myth.[2] More complex issues are under scrutiny than simply Yeats's repudiation of Christianity. Surely, one of those issues has to do with Yeats's *A Vision* and his attempt therein to create a modern mythology. Before he can create the new mythology, the old one must be upset. As Henn says, "The key word of the poem, twice repeated, is *unsatisfied*" ("The Green" 50). If the Magi are not satisfied with what they find at Calvary and its aftermath, it is worth noting Yeats sees them "now as at all times," always the "pale unsatisfied ones." Yeats never sees them as satisfied. Thus, they must have been unsatisfied before Calvary, too. Implicitly, there is no miracle at any time; or, no miracle ultimately can satisfy. Significantly, too, the Magi attended Christ at his birth, not at his death; here they seem more closely connected to the grave than to the cradle because Calvary is where Christ was crucified. If they are "unsatisfied" now, as they have been "at all times" in the poet's mind's eye, the Magi's search after wisdom has never ended or begun. The search has always been in the process of beginning, always underway, yet never really underway at all.

Yeats is making a statement about art and how art shapes our existence. The poem may actually illustrate the artist's search. The aesthetic imagination becomes personified as the "pale unsatisfied ones." Bohlman asserts that the "stiff, painted clothes" are equivalent to constricting Christianity (177). However, the "stiff, painted clothes" are images occupying the "mind's eye," details from a vast aesthetic reservoir. The Magi's "ancient faces like rain-beaten stones" is not just a description of the old, searching men, but a description of those ancient emblems belonging to the cultural consciousness. The "faces" are not just old, they are time-eroded; they lose significance because culture is erosive. The emblems do not belong to the historical world, where Christianity has its expression, but to the aesthetic world of the imagination. The appearance and disappearance of the Magi in "the blue depth of sky" is like the artist's crossing of real and imaginative borders.[3]

Yeats leaves the Magi unsatisfied. Leaving the search unfulfilled is consistent to Yeats's poetic designs. If everything is entwined, as it often is in Yeats's verse, everything is simultaneously unsatisfied and satisfied. For example, Fergus, who chooses to leave the easy life of being king, takes on the responsibility of wisdom; he believes wisdom will lead him to a happier existence, but he discovers wisdom is a greater, sadder burden than the easy life. Yet, he is the joyful master of his tragic world. In the example of "The Magi," the wise men are perhaps satisfied being unsatisfied because the search makes their existence significant. They give meaning to their own lives because they search, and their persistence makes the search significant. Analogously, the aesthetic creation may satisfy the artist; however, this satisfaction does not keep the artist from creating again. The artist keeps searching and, perhaps, for the same reason as the Magi.

The comedy of "The Dolls" may be read within this antithetical unity. In "The Dolls," a doll, emblematic of art, is offended by the presence of the baby, emblematic of nature. The doll rages, "That is an insult to us." The "oldest of all the dolls," "being kept for show," had seen "generations of [the baby's] sort" and "outscreams the whole shelf." Its complaint is that there is no evil in the doll-maker's house, yet "the man and the woman bring / Hither, to our disgrace, / A noisy and filthy thing." A study of the final lines is worthwhile:

> Hearing him groan and stretch
> The doll-maker's wife is aware

Her husband has heard the wretch,
And crouched by the arm of his chair,
She murmurs into his ear,
Head upon shoulder leant:
'My dear, my dear, O dear,
It was an accident.'

Who is "the wretch"? We assume it is the baby, the "noisy and filthy thing." However, it might be "the oldest of all the dolls" because it screams loudest. It seems the most wretched of anyone in this particular scene. Nothing indicates that the baby, at this particular moment, is making any noise at all. The dolls are the screaming and bawling creatures. The inversion of the natural and the unnatural (or aesthetic) is important because it raises questions about what kind of dolls these are and who the doll-maker is.

The answer to these considerations is found in Yeats's metapoetics. The poem is a parable or analogy of the poet's relationship to the poetic art. The dolls are emblems of the artist's craft; if they rage, they rage against the natural world. The artist, meanwhile, belongs to the natural world and to the world of artifice. He not only fathers dolls but children. When he begins to "groan and stretch" to wake, it is either the natural world or the world of artifice that wakes him. Both dolls and baby, and what they are emblems of, are all entwined in the metaphor for art. The natural world cannot escape the unnatural, and the unnatural cannot escape the natural.

The doll-maker's wife plays a significant role because she acts as intermediary between the world of art and the world of nature. The dolls, if they are emblematic of art, represent aesthetic design, the deliberate plan for creation; however, the baby, which "was an accident," represents the chance of creation in nature. The artist, clearly, is positioned between both worlds. The tyranny of art, as illustrated by the shouting dolls, would demand complete obeisance from the artist were it not for the wife's presence. She "*murmurs* into his ear" (emphasis added), keeping him calmed by the seductions of bodily life. Though tyrannical, art cannot be separated from the natural world; art would be a mirror without a reflection if it were. The wife, instinctively, reconciles the artist to both the natural and the aesthetic worlds.

Another metapoetic poem is "A Coat." The poem begins: "I made my song a coat." The poem is something worn: the poet wears it in the imagination, and others who read the poem regard it as the poet's clothing. But when Yeats writes that he adorned this coat "with embroideries / Out of old mythologies / From heel to throat," he suggests the adornment of poetry with a gaudy sense of detail is inappropriate for poetry. As Peterson puts it, "[T]he poet directly expresses his dissatisfaction with the embroidered song of his youth, caught and worn by fools" (98). Part of the problem with such detail is that "the fools caught it, / Wore it in the world's eyes / As though they'd wrought it." They imitate rather than create; thus, their art is false. Imitation reduces the pleasure of the original; therefore, "there's more enterprise / In walking naked." Walking naked, alluding perhaps to the emperor's new clothes, is how art should be. As Ellmann notes, Yeats "did not mean that he would give up his early symbols, but that the elements, for example, would from now on be part of his skin instead of part of his outer garments" (*Identity* 38).

Since art is part of Yeats's "outer skin," art as a subject for poetry is an act of walking naked. Readers who understand this should not be surprised or dismayed by its frequency in Yeats's poetry, nor should they stumble over the more difficult metapoetic pieces, such as "The Statues" and "The Gyres." Bloom, who calls "The Statues" "a cluttered, arrogant poem," finds much fault in it because, I think, he does not understand well enough the self-reflexiveness of the metaphor of art. Bloom says, "A poet of enormous gifts can meditate endlessly upon a vital matter, and still compose less than a great poem, if his own prejudices, fashionable and unfashionable, prevent his full humanity from entering into the meditation" (441). Bloom misses his mark when he addresses the poet's "full humanity." The body of Yeats's poetry is his attempt to discover what full humanity is, not a single poem. His aesthetic vision draws him close to full humanity, but the vision of what it is to be human fades rapidly. How can Yeats bring "his full humanity" into a poem if the ideal is still elusive? At best, the poetic search draws him into the Unity of Being; it creates for him a temporary, ecstatic wholeness; but, wholeness also eludes the poet almost as soon as it arrives. Search and meditation are vital to the poet, certainly, yet through search and meditation "*full* humanity" (emphasis added) can never be found. No human can ever discover fullness. The best any poet can do is create a tenuous approximation.

"The Statues" is a poetic study about humanity's search through art for perfection, that thing Bloom called "full humanity." However, "The Statues" is not a poem about "full humanity"; the search would be pointless if it were. Art, itself, would be purposeless if we knew what "full humanity" was. The poet asks, "Why did the people stare?" "[T]hough they moved or seemed to move," Pythagoras's designs "lacked character" and seem hardly worth the notice. Still, something in the art of the statues arrests attention. Even

> boys and girls pale from the imagined love
> Of solitary beds knew what they were,
> That passion could bring character enough;
> And pressed at midnight in some public place
> Live lips upon a plummet-measured face.

Though the statues "lacked character," the statue's viewers and the boys and girls understood how human passion transfers to the inanimate. Boys and girls, in adolescent fantasy, kiss or hug a pillow, pretending it is the object of their love; they may press "live lips upon a plummet-measured face" for the same reason. Human passion makes the inanimate come alive in the imaginative image, making the thing attractive. That passionate impulse is certainly belonging to the anima bruta metaphor; but, it also belongs to the metaphor for art. Granted, "The Statues" is problematic; many of its allusions are difficult. Though obscure, virtually all of these allusions pertain to art. Stanza two, for example, discusses how "the men / That with a mallet or a chisel modelled these / Calculations that look but casual flesh" brought an end to Asian aesthetic formlessness ("All Asiatic vague immensities"). This might suggest Yeats's own preference of form. But is it prejudice, as Bloom suggests? Not really, for poets forever endeavor to form experience; the mere shaping of a poem draws experience from its formlessness. To prefer form to formlessness is a matter of craft, not prejudice.

Consider, too, the poem's third stanza, which Bloom calls "a bad, crabbed stanza" (444):

> One image crossed the many-headed, sat
> Under the tropic shade, grew round and slow,
> No Hamlet thin from eating flies, a fat
> Dreamer of the Middle-Ages. Empty eye-balls knew
> That knowledge increases unreality, that
> Mirror on mirror mirrored is all the show.
> When gong and conch declare the hour to bless
> Grimalkin crawls to Buddha's emptiness.

Certainly, the stanza is difficult. The syntax is labored and the details obscure, but not as much so in the context of Yeats's other work. In Chapter One, I discussed "deliberate slowness." The difficulty of this particular stanza slows our reading, calls our attention to the words. The stanza demands deliberate reading and consideration because, if form is an extension of content, something valuable and difficultly gained is embedded here.

The "One image" of Buddha brings to mind similarities to Pythagoras's designs; as well, it alludes to the image of Buddha seen in "The Double Vision of Michael Robartes." The reference to Hamlet, though literary, brings to mind both western art and western humanity; furthermore, it creates juxtaposed estrangement, linked, as it is, to the eastern icon. Hamlet is an aberration from the aesthetic design of the statues. Modern civilization is concerned more with humanism than with aestheticism, thus the figure in art becomes more human, and tragically so. The more realistic humanity's representation becomes in art, the less we can transfer our own emotions to the work. What we respond to, then, is little more than our mirror image. Hamlet, for example, exemplifies modern humanity's dilemma: powerless to act, the individual is forced to action.[4] However, the "empty eye-balls" of the statues "knew / That knowledge increases unreality." Though blind, the statues possess knowledge about knowledge. Because the statues are outside humanity's wisdom, what they represent makes them more sublimely wise. Thus, when "gong and conch declare the hour to bless," the cat figure Grimalkin, Hamlet, and all of us, may crawl to Buddha's blesséd "emptiness." Curiously, Yeats's inclusion of the cat signifies an equivalence between animality and humanity. As I discussed in Chapter Three, the cat of "The Cat and the Moon" is "close kindred" to the moon, just as humanity is "close kindred" to God. In that poem, the cat's eyes were "changing." If the first parallel is valid, perhaps we might assert a second: humanity's eyes are "changing," too. The distinction between the cat's relationship to the moon and our relationship to God is our God's static quality. The moon changes, but God does not. Hence, humanity loses its kinship to God when the two cannot keep apace with each other; chaos ensues, and in that subsequent chaos we seek our solace elsewhere. Buddha's emptiness, its lack of expression and its form implicitly a vessel in which we might pour our passions, allows us to climb out of the wreck of our "formless, spawning, fury" of the "filthy modern tide." The "changing eyes" of Grimalkin and humanity look for reconcilement in the empty eyes of Buddha. Though empty, those eyes do not lack form, as the modern world does. The antinomies of blind calm and knowing confusion fuse and a pervading peace comes to us because we transfer our passions to the work of art. Specifically, though Buddha is diety, we embrace not the God but the representation of *God*. We may make of the artifact what we want it to be; however, in the "proper dark" of our instincts, we may "trace / The lineaments of a plummet-measured face" and, perhaps, rediscover our own character. Art's "empty eye-balls" do not judge; rather, art helps us to define who we are.

"The Gyres" is another example of Yeats's metapoetics. This poem's self-reflexiveness is due to its particular dependence upon *A Vision* and "The Second Coming." For example, the poem's first line, "The gyres! the gyres!," recalls the "Turning and turning" of the falcon and the reeling of the desert birds in "The Second Coming." These, of course, represent Yeats's concept of the intersecting cones that signal the beginning and ending of a cycle, as described in *A Vision*. The opening exclamation is not panic, but excitement. "Old Rocky Face look forth," the poet writes, drawing its attention to the end of an age. Bloom mistakenly assumes that Old Rocky Face is Yeats himself (435); rather, the persona of the poem addresses all the Rocky Faces in his world and of his poetry. The image calls to mind the moon of "The Cat and the Moon."

Is not the moon, locked in its unalterable orbit, a Rocky Face? Does that moon not suggest both god and humanity?[5] Might it refer to the Sphinx in both "The Double Vision of Michael Robartes" and "The Second Coming"? The poem is exultant because it proves to all disbelieving Rocky Faces that the gyres confirm the ensuing change. As metapoetic emblems, the gyres illustrate how art makes tangible the intangible. They illustrate through aesthetic design the world's impermanence, how

> Things thought too long can be no longer thought
> For beauty dies of beauty, worth of worth,
> And ancient lineaments are blotted out.
> Irrational streams of blood are staining earth;
> Empedocles has thrown all things about;
> Hector is dead and there's a light in Troy;
> We that look on but laugh in tragic joy.

If the gyres confirm the universe's upheaval, art and its inherent design make clear to us our ensuing chaos. Those who understand the power of metaphor know a new set of emblems will assert themselves, antithetically recreating the world.

When Yeats twice asks, "What matter?" he makes his point well understood. The end of an age does not matter. We should not sigh or cry because "a greater, a more gracious time has gone," for the present time will pass, too. This implies, of course, that the antithesis to the current, inhospitable and more inferior time will be a "greater," "more gracious time" to come. The persona says he had sighed once, "but not again," because "Out of Cavern comes a voice / And all it knows is that one word 'Rejoice.'"

The "Out of Cavern" reference is interesting because it might allude to numerous sources. For example, in *A Vision* Yeats writes about "the Christian primary dispensation, the child born in the Cavern" (204). If we stop reading here, we might misinterpret the voice saying, "Rejoice!" as Christ's. However, Yeats proceeds: "At or near the central point of our civilisation must come antithetical revelation, the turbulent child of the Altar" (*Vision* 204). In the note to this passage, Yeats writes, "I am thinking of the two symbols discovered by Frobenius in Africa, the Cavern, symbol of the nations moving westward, the Altar at the centre of radiating roads, symbol of the nations moving eastward" (*Vision* 204). If Christian dispensation was symbolized by the Cavern, the Cavern is symbolic of western culture and its reliance upon principles of morality and reason. The Altar, however, suggests an opposite movement, not necessarily toward immorality, but at least a direction from the constraints and shackles of Christianity. The two symbols of Cavern and Altar are, in a sense, gyres. Thus, the voice might belong to the unnamed "child of the Altar." Then again, Yeats gives us another possibility in his *Autobiography*.

> I now know that there are men who cannot possess "Unity of Being," who must not seek it or express it—and who, so far from seeking an anti-self, a Mask that delineates a being in all things the opposite to their natural state, can but seek the suppression of the anti-self, till the natural state alone remains. These are those who must seek no image of desire, but await that which lies beyond their mind—unities not of the mind, but unities of nature, unities of God—the man of science, the moralist, the humanitarian, the politician, St. Simon Stylites upon his pillar, St. Anthony in his cavern, all whose preoccupation is to seem nothing, to summon a creator by revealing chaos, to become the lamp for another's wick and oil; and indeed it may be that it has been for their guidance in a very special sense that the "perfectly proportioned human body" suffered crucifixion. (166)

Perhaps, then, the voice of the cavern is St. Anthony's. However, if St. Anthony is one of those who wants "to seem nothing," the command to rejoice contradicts that "preoccupation." "Rejoice" would be an "image of desire." Consequently, the voice is certainly neither Christ's nor St. Anthony's, for these have one fundamental difference from the text of "The Gyres." The Christ child is *in* the cavern; St. Anthony is *in* the cavern. In "The Gyres," the voice is "Out of Cavern." Most readers would assume this as a voice from out of the cavern, that it is a voice *in* the cavern that we, on the outside, can hear. However, because Yeats capitalizes *out*, we likely ought to read it emphatically; this emphasis places the voice on the outside of the cavern while it may, implicitly, place us in it. After all, what purpose does rejoicing have but to bring us out of darkness? Therefore, readers who tend to misconstrue the voice that knows but one word, "Rejoice," ought to look somewhere other than these sources.

I suggest we first examine what *cavern* means. The cavern suggests darkness, something subterranean and mysterious, something labyrinthine. Christ and St. Anthony belong to that labyrinthine world. Further, *cavern* suggests *nothing*, a void or vast emptiness. Thus, Yeats has assigned Christianity to an existential abyss. But the rejoicing voice is out of the cavern; it has exited the dark labyrinth into whatever new light the gyres bring. As metapoetry, the voice "Out of Cavern" may well be the poet's voice; the purpose of poetry may be to "reveal chaos," but only by the release of the aesthetic imagination from its labyrinth.

In the final stanza of the poem, Yeats repeats the affirmative "What matter!" "Those that Rocky Face holds dear" will "disinter / The workman, noble and saint" from their tombs and their "dark nothing," and everything will "run / On that unfashionable gyre again." The gyres, and the imagination, ensure a sort of eternity: what existed will exist again because of their workings. All that are committed to the "dark nothing" of the Cavern will come out of it. The poetic consciousness is also Cavern; therefore, the voice is jubilant because the mind has let out an image. Once the imaginative image stands in revelatory light, we can see that things pass and are made new again, that those who have died are once again living. The metaphor for art brings us joy in the eternity of our resurrected imaginings.

When Yeats writes such poems as "The Statues" and "The Gyres," he has moved well beyond the metaphors for art found in "The Song of the Happy Shepherd" and "Adam's Curse." He is not so much concerned with what art *is* any longer as he is with what art does. The distinction, however, does not suggest Yeats has given up his original concepts. Rather, the "certain good" of words, the labor of the poetic process, the curse and blessing of the poetic dance, become the vehicle for the metapoetical story: of how art lets us cling to all the "fine things"; how art and nature are inseparable; how art keeps us pursuing answers to our existential riddle; and how, ultimately, we rise, because of art, from our dark caverns into light.

Chapter 5

Yeats's Tower: The Metaphor of the Aesthetic Intelligence

The story of the poem about what art is and does is prevalent in Yeats's work. Sometimes, however, Yeats's metapoetics had to do with writers and their community and with the poet's perception of the universe. This change from solely aesthetic principles to what becomes contiguous poetic territory is significant because it represents a transitional phase for Yeats's metaphors for art. In this phase, Yeats leaves behind questions about what art is and what art does in order to examine the aesthetic intelligence or psyche. Specifically, the metaphor for the aesthetic intelligence is architecture.

The two principal transitional pieces are "Coole Park, 1929" and "Coole Park and Ballylee, 1931." In the earlier poem, Yeats begins,

> I meditate upon a swallow's flight,
> Upon an aged woman and her house,
> A sycamore and lime tree lost in night
> Although that western cloud is luminous,
> Great works constructed there in nature's spite
> For scholars and for poets after us,
> Thoughts long knitted into a single thought,
> A dance-like glory that those walls begot.

A particularly important structural metaphor occurs here because it shapes the majority of Yeats's architectural pieces. The first line points the poet's and our eyes skyward. The aesthetic intelligence communes with the "swallow's flight," and, in this communion, the mind's eye also sees "an aged woman and her house." The poetic flight, equivalent to the swallow's, places us in intangible air only to lead us to an earthbound, tangible subject. This pattern of juxtaposition of contraries is subsequently inverted in the next line: "sycamore and lime tree," though earthbound, reach upward to the night where they are lost. However, because Yeats's aesthetic intelligence understands the reconciliatory nature of opposites, it finds the "luminous" cloud of revelation in the night sky. This revelation draws us earthward, again, to meditate upon Lady Gregory's artistry, upon her beneficience to scholars and poets, and upon the aesthetic environment her house creates.

This last point is worth repeating because it captures the essence of Yeats's architectural metaphor: the house creates an aesthetic environment no less than a poet's psyche does. Furthermore, though our poetic flight might send us temporarily into the ethereal world, it nonetheless lands us on earth where our real subjects for art exist. The metaphorical pattern in Yeats's architectural poems most often illustrates the aesthetic intelligence initially elevated; however, the natural world where art must occur draws our attention from the intangible to concrete. The artistic impulse may be, at first, to soar into space, but flight obviously belongs to creatures of nature and all the earthliness that natural existence involves.

In *Eminent Domain*, Ellmann discusses the relationship of art and nature. He writes:

> For Yeats art and nature have more revelations to offer, and art is essentially a dialectic between nature—whether revelatory or not—and what Kant calls "second nature," the artist's own creation from elements nature supplies. This dialectic considers many possibilities, that art depends upon nature, that it interpenetrates nature, that it is powerless in nature, that it shapes nature (as Wilde liked to say), that it transcends nature, and it conceives of nature variously as a temple of symbols or as what Stevens calls "one insoluble lump" without ulterior meaning. (116)

In metapoetry, particularly, the "second nature" may indeed be the poet's "creation from elements nature supplies." Lady Gregory's residence provided Yeats much, as did the aesthetic community there. Naturally, then, Yeats uses these elements to illustrate Coole Park. Equally natural, he uses as subject the elements of poetry generated by the Coole Park experience. Yeats's initial focus upon Lady Gregory and her house suggests that she, as artist, and her house, as art-generating artifact, provided Yeats his "dialectic between nature" and "second nature." Directly, she joined art to nature by making her home a bower or nest for other artists.

This "nest image," reinforced by the "sycamore and lime tree," seems reasonable when Yeats establishes his artist-as-bird metaphor in the following stanza. The poets

> came like swallows and like swallows went,
> And yet a woman's powerful character
> Could keep a swallow to its first intent;
> And half a dozen in formation there,
> That seemed to whirl upon a compass-point,
> Found certainty upon the dreaming air, . . .

Bloom notes that "[t]hese poetical birds hear their keeper," unlike the falcon of "The Second Coming." Thus, Lady Gregory and her home are the "reverse" of the pattern we see in that poem (381). Bloom continues: "The poem's impressive meaning is that for these writers and men of culture . . . things did not fall apart, because Lady Gregory maintained the ceremony of innocence, or at least enough of it so that true work could be done" (381). This is a good reading of the poem, for clearly things are well in this environment. Lady Gregory is, in many respects, "a compass-point" that the artists look to for direction. Art is dependent upon Lady Gregory's good nature; she helps to define the "certainty upon the dreaming air" of artistic pursuit. She helps the artists to discover what is concrete and tangible as subject for art in the "dreaming" portions of the aesthetic intelligence.

But if nature is a metaphor for art here, so is Lady Gregory's home. Psychological readings often equate the structure of a house to the structure of the human psyche. In this case, the home is a metaphor for the artistic imagination. While all is well with the house, all is well for art and for the community of artists. However, the final stanza ponders what will transpire when the place has been left to ruin:

> Here, traveller, scholar, poet, take your stand
> When all those rooms and passages are gone,
> When nettles wave upon a shapeless mound
> And saplings root among the broken stone,
> And dedicate—eyes bent upon the ground,
> Back turned upon the brightness of the sun
> And all the sensuality of the shade—
> A moment's memory to that laurelled head.

If the house is a metaphor for art, the imagination is left in disarray and sorrowful, reverent state once the house is gone. The imagination becomes "a shapeless mound," an empty lot. Notice how we no longer cast our eyes skyward; they are "bent upon the ground" toward "the sensuality of the shade." We are, in many ways, looking upon a grave. However, at no other point in this poem are the details simultaneously so physical and sensuous.

If "Coole Park, 1929" leaves us on a rather somber note, despite its initial celebratory theme, "Coole Park and Ballylee, 1931" pulls us deeper into a pervading sense of somberness. Bloom would disagree; he says, "Though still celebratory, it celebrates in high desperation" (381). Frankly, if the poem is celebratory, it celebrates past glory and not the glory coming. Here, the poet cannot conceive what glory could exist when this particular world is shattered by Lady Gregory's impending death. If Yeats celebrates, the celebration might be found in the third through fifth stanzas:

> That stormy white
> But seems a concentration of the sky;
> And, like the soul, it sails into the sight
> And in the morning's gone, no man knows why;
> And is so lovely that it sets to right
> What knowledge or its lack had set awry,
> So arrogantly pure, a child might think
> It can be murdered with a spot of ink.
>
> Sound of a stick upon the floor, a sound
> From somebody that toils from chair to chair;
> Beloved books that famous hands have bound,
> Old marble heads, old pictures everywhere;
> Great rooms where travelled men and children found
> Content or joy; a last inheritor
> Where none has reigned that lacked a name and fame
> Or out of folly into folly came.
>
> A spot whereon the founders lived and died
> Seemed once more dear than life; ancestral trees
> Of gardens rich in memory glorified
> Marriages, alliances and families,
> And every bride's ambition satisfied.
> Where fashion or mere fantasy decrees
> Man shifts about—all that great glory spent
> Like some poor Arab tribesman and his tent.

Surely, Lady Gregory's home deserves praise—the memories it evokes are worthy of exultation. However, these do not adequately offset the details of disillusionment. The grammar of these three sections relies heavily upon the use of past tense verbs: *have bound*; *found*; *reigned*; *lacked*; *lived*; *died*; *seemed*; *glorified*; *satisfied*; *spent*. These all suggest that what once transpired at Coole is gone, except in memory. Coupled to these verbs are others that suggest the very act of something passing: *seems*; *sails*; *is gone*; *can be murdered*; *toils*; *decrees*; *shifts*. The only affirmative, positive, future-pointing verbs are found in the third stanza, where the "stormy white" of the "flooded lake" "*is* so lovely that it *sets* to right / What knowledge or its lack had set awry" (emphasis added). Affirmative, and contradictory to "had set," these are nonetheless sandwiched between many implicitly negative verb-constructions. Desperate emotions exist because things are wrong at Coole; the house is in decline because Lady Gregory, illustrated making her way across the room ("Sound of a stick upon the floor, a sound / From somebody that toils from chair to chair"), is in decline.

If the old woman who held things together in "Coole Park, 1929" is failing, the prophetic vision of the poet who foretold its ruin must now record ruin's results in "Coole Park and Ballylee, 1931." While the poet recalls the way things were years before, undeniably "all is changed." If the woman falls, the house falls; metaphorically, if the house falls, the imagination must mirror the details of the fall. As a metaphor for art, the house in shambles mirrors the shambles of the nature surrounding the poet, the nature of the poet's imagination, and the nature that once bound the Coole Park artists together.

When Yeats writes, "Under my window-ledge the waters race, / Otters below and moor-hens on the top," he is literally speaking about the waters near his tower at Ballylee. The window-ledge is literal enough, too; however, metaphorically, it belongs to the house of his imagination. Just as the actual waters of the stream near his tower darken and "run underground," the poet's imaginative waters (bringing to mind Coleridge's "Kubla Khan") run their underground course before they "rise in a rocky place." The rocky place, also a literal description, is simultaneously the poet's unsettled state of mind, resultant from Lady Gregory's failing health. Furthermore, Yeats says, "What's water but the generated soul?"; certainly, metaphorically, he is correct. When the imagination moves, it is a stream; when it rises "in a rocky place," the imagination stops moving and becomes a lake, a pool of consciousness. As if Yeats fears our misunderstanding this concept, he self-consciously reiterates the point in the second stanza:

> Upon the border of that lake's a wood
> Now all dry sticks under a wintry sun,
> And in a copse of beeches there I stood,
> For Nature's pulled her tragic buskin on

And all the rant's a mirror of my mood: . . .

Both Nature and poet rant over Lady Gregory's tragedy. Significantly, too, the reference to the dry sticks here rebounds upon the synecdoche of the "sound of a stick upon the floor." These are emblems of nature's cyclical aging, of winter and death coming on.

The metaphor of art records the loss of Lady Gregory and the loss of a particular kind of art. "We were the last romantics," Yeats writes, implying their day has passed. Bloom faults this final section because he misreads Yeats's concept of romanticism.[1] Even so, the themes of the romantics—"traditional sanctity and loveliness," "whatever's written in what poets name / The book of the people," "whatever most can bless / The mind of man or elevate a rhyme"—are gone because "all is changed." It no longer matters that Homer once rode his "high horse" where now "the swans drift upon a darkening flood." For these Romantics, the swan, emblematic of "whatever most can bless," will be lost in the undercurrents of life's "darkening flood" after Coole Park. Its demise is equivalent to the demise of that generation and that generation's poetry.

Another point of comparison between "Coole Park and Ballylee, 1931" and "Coole Park, 1929" merits further study, too. The same structural metaphor found in the earlier poem occurs in the later. In the first stanza, the poet, quite literally, is elevated; he is in his tower, while under him, in the stream, are "otters below and moor-hens on the top." The "above-below" pattern is repeated in the juxtaposition of "Heaven's face" to "'dark' Raftery's 'cellar.'" In the second stanza, we find the inversion of the pattern; poetic vision concentrates upon the "wood / Now all dry sticks under a wintry sun," but in the "thunder of the mounting swan" the eyes move upward "where the branches break / The glittering reaches of the flooded lake." Furthermore, the image of the lake at the end of the second stanza transforms into "that stormy white" which "seems a concentration of the sky." Yet this "concentration," "a child might think," "can be murdered with a spot of ink," and we are earthbound, again. We are left in Lady Gregory's physical and decaying world throughout the remainder of the poem. "All is changed" because of this transference from elevated place to earthly one. The "last romantics" might have tried to "elevate a rhyme" once; clearly, the architectural metaphor illustrates it cannot happen this way any longer.

The same structural pattern recurs in virtually all of Yeats's architectural poems. Furthermore, in each instance Yeats employs this pattern, we discover through the juxtaposition of upstairs and ground floor significant tensions. "In Memory of Major Robert Gregory," for example, illustrates how the tower is a metaphor for the psyche, and how memories rise from the unconscious to conscious mind. This equivalent is simple enough; however, in Yeats's architecture, things are perhaps calmer in the lower recesses of the tower. Yeats writes:

> Now that we're almost settled in our house
> I'll name the friends that cannot sup with us
> Beside a fire of turf in th' ancient tower,
> And having talked to some late hour
> Climb up the narrow winding stair to bed:
> Discoveries of forgotten truth
> Or mere companions of my youth,
> All, all are in my thoughts to-night being dead.

If the tower is a metaphor for the psyche, part of the poet's life is "almost settled," too. But the word *almost* is the crux of this stanza; *almost* implies *not.* Although Yeats's friends are dead and cannot join him "beside a fire of turf in th' ancient tower," they are nonetheless present in the ancient tower of the collective, though troubled memory. Metaphorically, the climbing of "the narrow winding stair to bed" is equivalent to the resurfacing of his friend's images from unconscious to conscious mind; this is the manner in which imagination functions. Though the friends are dead, they are very much alive in the poet's mind. Hence, the tower metaphor disinters their bodies, allowing Yeats to celebrate them through words for the next nine stanzas.

Although Yeats leaves the architectural metaphor after the first stanza, he revives it in the final two. Stanza XI addresses how some "may consume / The entire combustible world in one small room." The furnace image evokes the metaphorical image of the imaginative fires, the fires of poetic inspiration. "The bare chimney is gone black out" refers not only, literally, to the loss of the friends, as if they were fires gone out, but also to the frightening aspect that loss of such friends may equal the extinguishing of poetic fires. Significantly, the final architectural metaphor of "In Memory of Major Robert Gregory" is a window. When the poet writes "how bitter is that wind / That shakes the shutter," we may accept this literally. However, the architectural metaphor suggests the window is an opening to the poet's imagination. Thus, the wind may be a metaphorical wind that shakes the poet, making him *shudder*, causing him to lose focus upon the "appropriate commentary" about his friends. If this is so, that wind may be the ethereal airs of inspiration beating upon the closed shutters of the poet's consciousness. Though the winds are nonetheless intrusive, the poet does not want these winds to blow freely because they would be "inappropriate" to his aesthetic, more tangible task.

This last comment raises a significant point about the architectural metaphor. Just as Yeats was able to soar to fairyland through his imagination, through art he is able to construct architectural walls to stay the unpleasant world. However, each time Yeats builds his metaphorical paradises or houses, the outside world disturbs the vision. It gets inside, and the quiet stay for the poet is always tenuous and temporary. This is not a pathetic thing, though. Certainly, imprisonment in a hostile universe is tragic; however, the construction of these metaphors allows the imaginative mind an embrace, however temporary it may be, of something permanent. The world may come to its ruin, but the reservoir of vision is always intact. As Engelberg notes, in many respects Yeats is a "master builder who rearranges with his 'mythy mind'—to borrow a phrase from Wallace Stevens—the fictive world becomes real" ("Arcadia" 87).

Of course, even the "fictive world" has its problems. "In Memory of Major Robert Gregory" reflects the poet's troubled imagination, as does "A Prayer for My Daughter":

> I have walked and prayed for this young child an hour
> And heard the sea-wind scream upon the tower,
> And under the arches of the bridge, and scream
> In the elms above the flooded stream;
> Imagining in excited reverie
> That the future years had come,
> Dancing to a frenzied drum,
> Out of the murderous innocence of the sea.

The howling storm may not equal the storm in the poet's mind, but it certainly awakes that storm. Thus, when Yeats writes his paradise and house poems, he strives toward the ideal sanctum but generally falls somewhat short of the ideal. Again, I do not believe this is failure of the poet nor of the poetry; Yeats would consider this a heroic gesture, such as Cuchulain's fight with the invulnerable sea. That he succeeds is ultimately not as important as the effort to succeed. Unity of Being may be impossible, but the struggle draws the poet nearer perfection. As Edward Lense says, "For Yeats, the Other World in any of the forms he gave it was the expression of one emotion, a concentration of feeling entirely different from the partial and shifting emotions of this world" (95). This one emotion, I think, is Yeats's expression of heroic courage in the face of the mutable, malevolent world. The actual tower or house may succumb to time's erosive powers, but the metaphor becomes an irreducible image in the poet's mind.

In other "tower" poems, Yeats examines the architectural metaphor more closely. The first of these, "The Tower," illustrates a number of metaphorical points. In the first section, Yeats writes,

> What shall I do with this absurdity—

O heart, O troubled heart—this caricature,
Decrepit age that has been tied to me
As to a dog's tail?

Here, "absurdity" is equivalent to the "caricature" of "decrepit age." Though he is old, his heart is yearning and youthful. The poet writes,

Never had I more
Excited, passionate, fantastical
Imagination, nor an ear and eye
That more expected the impossible . . . .

However, the reader must wonder: is this a poem about Yeats or about the tower, as the title suggests? Certainly, the poem is about both; what may not be readily understood, however, is that images of the poet and tower are metaphorically entwined. Like the poet, the tower is old; and, where the poet still has "excited, passionate, fantastical / Imagination," the tower has its unaging permanence.

Both tower and body may fall to ruin, but the aesthetic intelligence is obviously sound and productive in the symbol and in the poet's imagination. Ironically, excitement, passion, and fantasy have everything to do with the aging poet. When Yeats says "it *seems*" (emphasis added) he "must bid the Muse go pack" and content himself "with argument and deal / In abstract things," he is really stating that such poetic direction would be an unacceptable course; the alternative, to "be derided by / A sort of battered kettle at the heel," a repetition of the image of "decrepit age" tied to a dog's tail, would actually be the preferred direction. The first section of "The Tower" ends upon the puzzlement of this irony. At one level, the tower is a metaphor of the poet's self-mockery and uselessness. The images remain permanent and whole, but derisive and erosive age contradict human perfection. On another level, the tower metaphor suggests the antithetical qualities of art: while art may deride life's imperfections, art may be, nonetheless, an attainable perfection; it does not erode. Yeats puzzles over the contradictions between perfect image and imperfect physical world. Reasonably, Yeats will lead us through the poem, maintaining the tower metaphor, until he comes to liveable terms with the "absurdity" of his own existence as well as, perhaps, the absurdity of his metaphor. After all, the tower ought to provide some sort of protection; the tenant ought to be able to climb to its top to stave off the warring beneath him. In Yeats's case, the uppermost portion of his metaphor has him considering as subject "abstract things" rather than the "battered kettles" of his existence. That position does not make him "content."

Thus, in the first line of the second stanza, Yeats writes, "I pace upon the battlements." Literally, these are the battlements of the tower; metaphorically, they are battlements within his mind as it works out his antithetical dilemma. Notice where the poet focuses his attention; though he is at the top of the tower, with full and attentive consciousness, he seeks his answers at the bottom of the structure. He writes that he stares

> On the foundations of a house, or where
> Tree, like a sooty finger, starts from the earth;
> And send imagination forth
> Under the day's declining beam, and call
> Images and memories
> From ruin or from ancient trees,
> For I would ask a question of them all.

We can read this section literally enough; however, if the tower is a metaphor for the poet's imagination, these images have everything to do with imaginative process and not with the natural world. Yeats very nearly tells us this is so, for "the foundations of a house" and the shoots of the "tree, like a sooty finger" are the things that "send imagination forth." Aesthetic sensibility commences here. Because these are the foundations and roots of the imagination, they "call / Images and memories / From ruin or from ancient trees," the emblems of the collective consciousness, reservoir of myth, of allusion, of memory. As Yeats says many lines later, those images are "in the Great Memory stored."

Furthermore, Yeats says he "would ask a question" of all that is brought to mind. This begins a reverie on the history of the tower as well as on the personal history of the poet. Nine stanzas pass before we ever land upon a question, and then Yeats asks two. The first of these questions is,

> Did all old men and women, rich and poor,
> Who trod upon these rocks or passed this door,
> Whether in public or in secret rage
> As I do now against old age?

The second question is equally self-conscious, reminding us again of his failed love of Maud Gonne. He writes, "Does imagination dwell the most / Upon a woman won or woman lost?"[2] The first answer is obvious enough. Yeats writes, "I have found an answer in those eyes / That are impatient to be gone." Impatience belongs to youth, for "those eyes" do not commiserate with the aging poet.[3] If there is no patience for the poet, there is no patience for other "old men and women," either. The logical conclusion is that all old folks rage against age. The second answer is equally obvious, as is the pun of *gone*. We must assume the imagination dwells most upon the lost woman because Yeats omits any discussion upon the one won. What he says about the one lost is, at best, ironic:

> If on the lost, admit you turned aside
> From a great labyrinth out of pride,
> Cowardice, some silly over-subtle thought
> Or anything called conscience once;
> And that if memory recur, the sun's
> Under eclipse and the day blotted out.

I am taken by the suggestion of the labyrinth. Love and the object of love get us lost in a labyrinth; failure at love makes us avoid it because of "pride," "cowardice," "thought," and "conscience." If this is so, we who fail at love become less proud and more courageous because we must embrace our failure of will and courage; we become more speculative, reflective, and reasonable where, perhaps, we were once silly. Are these fair assumptions? Ironically, Yeats makes these things seem uncommendable qualities and implies the labyrinth is better. These failures, surely, caused Yeats to fear the labyrinth of love; however, I think it unlikely he would have done anything different. As he wrote in "A Dialogue of Self and Soul," "I am content to live it all again / And yet again." Thus, on one hand, Yeats probably never completely stopped loving Maud Gonne; on the other, he maybe never completely gave over to loving her, either. Regardless, she may be lost in one sense, but she is not lost in the imagination. The tower in the poet's mind, when it houses memories of the woman lost, becomes a labyrinth out of which Yeats must emerge through his poetry. The notion that such memories will put the sun "under eclipse" and make "the day blotted out" is additional irony. Reality may be blocked out, but revelation of self is not. The day is under eclipse, not the imagination. Running the labyrinth is worthwhile, even if the run takes place in the self-exposing imagination. Furthermore, these labyrinthine images arise from the foundation and the roots Yeats mentioned at the beginning of this section.

In section III, we find another image brought to the top of the imaginative tower:

> Death and life were not
> Till man made up the whole,
> Made lock, stock and barrel
> Out of his bitter soul,
> Aye, sun and moon and star, all,
> And further add to that
> That, being dead, we rise,

Dream and so create
Translunar Paradise.

Out of the recesses of the "Great Memory" comes Yeats's concept of eternity. Death is something man "made up" "out of his bitter soul." In the universal scheme of Yeats's "unfashionable gyres," dead humanity will rise again. Because of this, we can "dream and so create / Translunar Paradise," a visionary realm beyond the celestial. This is Yeats's notion of Unity of Being, again, what it is we have to be joyful about even in tragedy. Yeats repeats these sentiments in "Death": "He knows death to the bone— / Man has created death." Even that poem carries with it a sense of Yeatsian resurrection: "Many times he died, / Many times rose again." Nonetheless, we are brought up from our foundations to discover these truths in the tower of our minds.

In "Nineteen Hundred and Nineteen," the poet, viewing his world from his imaginative tower, reiterates a point made in "The Tower." He writes that "a man in his own secret meditation / Is lost amid the labyrinth that he has made / In art or politics." This time the labyrinth is not the result of lost love but of meditation upon art and politics. For Yeats, these are fundamental things—bricks in a foundation. He loses himself in a maze of his own making. Furthermore, the often quoted last stanza of section III illustrates how imagination works:

The swan has leaped into the desolate heaven:
That image can bring wildness, bring a rage
To end all things, to end
What my laborious life imagined, even
The half-imagined, the half-written page;
O but we dreamed to mend
Whatever mischief seemed
To afflict mankind, but now
That winds of winter blow
Learn that we were crack-pated when we dreamed.

Like the swan, the image flies up into consciousness, a "desolate heaven." It seeks to finish, to repair, but the poet's imagination knows that it can do neither completely. The "desolate heaven" is, in some ways, equivalent to the "cold and rook-delighting heaven" ("The Cold Heaven"). When the poetic spirit or "ghost begins to quicken," and its images rise to consciousness, a contradictory phenomenon occurs. Art can only be expressed in conscious terms; art is valuable because of our cultural and speculative appraisal of it. However, we are also conscious of art's obvious failure to "mend / Whatever mischief seemed to afflict mankind." Art does much, as discussed in Chapter Four; but, art cannot deter humanity's destructive course.

The "winds of winter blow" while the aesthetic psyche does its work. Ironically, while current artists

> mock at the great
> That had such burdens on the mind
> And toiled so hard and late
> To leave some monument behind,
> Nor thought of the levelling wind,

the levelling wind blows, nonetheless. Archetypically, the wind is inspiration. However, this wind inspires nothing other than the destruction of the monuments humanity leaves behind. The tower and, as a metaphor of the aesthetic intelligence, the art that arises from it, may be wind-levelled monuments. The destructive wind counteracts the procreative winds of the poetic process. In Yeats's case, when the poet brings the poetic subject to consciousness, the wind seems always to tear at Yeats's tower. In "A Prayer for My Daughter," "the storm is howling" and the poet hears "the sea-wind scream upon the tower." "In Memory of Major Robert Gregory" illustrated "how bitter is that wind / That shakes the shutter." Surely, the wind is most portentous in the upper portions of the tower, at the conscious level. The failure of art is its inability to "bar that foul storm out," though its success must be that it has "leaped" nonetheless. Like Cuchulain who fights, though he cannot defeat the "invulnerable tide," the poet's art tends the individual wounds of the world's inhabitants, though it cannot heal the world itself. Though the image leaps into light, that light is surrounded by perpetual darkness.

In "A Dialogue of Self and Soul," the soul ascends "the winding ancient stair" to "fix every wandering thought upon / That quarter where all thought is done: / Who can distinguish darkness from the soul?" The Soul looks beyond the "broken, crumbling battlement" into space, that "Translunar Paradise." As Daniel Harris states,

> The mystical ascent proposed in "A Dialogue of Self and Soul" climaxes Yeats's fascination with the tower's top and what lies beyond it, the contemplative world of the spirit's perfection. Because the poem so emphatically polarizes the tower's base and top, Self's choice not to ascend appears all the more decisive. The poem is Yeats's most blunt, tragic affirmation of existence. (203)

Instead of ascending with the Soul, the Self stays below and finds its "blest" existence by following "to its source / Every event in action or in thought."

Truth begins at the bottom of the tower, not beyond its battlements. This concept Yeats repeats in "The Circus Animals' Desertion": "I must lie down where all the ladders start."

In "Blood and the Moon," which follows "A Dialogue of Self and Soul," Yeats calls the tower "a bloody, arrogant power." He says, "In mockery I have set / A powerful emblem up," "half dead at the top." Here, he repeats the "half-hid" image first noted in "A Prayer for My Daughter" and the futility of looking beyond the tower's top. Chatterjee notes,

> Almost immediately the waste room at the top of Thor Ballylee recalls the state of the modern nation—"half dead at the top" and the blessed tower becomes an emblem of mockery. Towards the end of the poem, the poet smells with horror the "odour of blood on the ancestral stair." The image of retreat and wisdom is shaken by life's turmoil and the blood of innocence leaves its stain on its visage. (111)

"Blood and the Moon" is not just mockery of the "state of the modern nation," as Yeats also mocks himself as artist. The poet who pursues darkness, as the Soul does in the previous poem, is "half dead at the top" of dreaming consciousness. More abundant life must be at the source, at the bottom of the winding stair.[5] The building of the architectural metaphor cannot begin, in other words, looking outward into the universe; it must be built as the tower is built, from ground up. Thus, if the Self wants to begin at the source, this is the way the imaginative process works. The original emblem may crumble, but it nonetheless allows the poet to rise from the depths of discovery to that "Translunar Paradise." The Self cannot begin at the battlements or beyond. The tower metaphor illustrates, conclusively, that though we reach imaginative heights we are still nevertheless connected to earth.

Even Yeats's last "tower" poem (and last poem, written one week before his death), "The Black Tower," repeats some of these fundamental ideas. *Black* connotes *death*, and death occupies much of this piece. The men who belong to the black tower "lack nothing that a soldier needs" and they are "oath-bound men." The oath, apparently, is to avoid bribery, threat, or rumor when their "own right king's forgotten." Mention of the "right" king is important because it is reminiscent of the Soul's outward search into darkness. There is no king there. Meanwhile,

> The tower's old cook that must climb and clamber
> Catching small birds in the dew of the morn
> When we hale men lie stretched in slumber
> Swears that he hears the great king's horn.

He wends his way upward, like the Soul did; but the "great king's horn," reminiscent of Christ's return at the Resurrection, is not to be believed.[6] The men who "lie stretched in slumber" like corpses know that the cook is "a lying hound" and they stand by that "oath-bound." If the Self has contented itself with the source, so have these men who are "in the tomb." Recall, too, the wind that Yeats was troubled by in "A Prayer for my Daughter." Here, the

> winds come up from the shore;
> They shake when the winds roar
> Old bones upon the mountain shake.

If the king is not in his heaven blowing his horn to resurrect the soldiers, the wind is the only thing disturbing the bones.

The importance of the tower cannot be dismissed when we study the architectural metaphor. As Chatterjee notes,

> The Tower symbol . . . takes on many other associations from other poems and represents the poet's torturous processes of thought. The "winding, grying, spiring" stair suggests that it requires effort and toil to clamber on and reinforces the image of "mysterious wisdom worn by toil"; the spiral imagery also signifies that the tower is a part of the revolving historical cycle. The reference to the famous figures in Irish history, Swift, Grattan, Burke and others makes the tower a symbol of tradition, of national heritage: Irish history becomes related to Time's unending march. Elsewhere it becomes a symbol of violence, and of blood-thirstiness.(111)

Chatterjee's appraisal is essentially correct; however, the one point relevant to this study is how the tower suggests the artistic process. But where does poetry go from here; where should it come from? It should follow the Self's example and the example of the dead soldiers, locating its paradise at the source of experience and not in the Heavens. Paradise comes from the spirings of the imagination, not from thoughts on abstractions found in "half-dead" consciousness.

If Yeats has been endeavoring all along to build himself a paradise, he comes closest to it in "Sailing to Byzantium" and "Byzantium." The Byzantium metaphor has many foundations, derived from Shelley, Milton, Tennyson, and Coleridge.[7] In particular, I believe Yeats owes a considerable indebtedness to "Kubla Khan." The Coleridgean paradigm shows us complete separation from the world will not work. Too much of the inhospitable world accompanies the imagination at all times. The wind pummels Yeats's tower. Yeats's plight is that something forever interrupts the poetic vision of perfection. The tower, though the poet builds it to save himself through art, cannot save the poet completely. The tower's "winding, gyring, spiring treadmill" of the "ancestral stair" always bears the "odour of blood" ("Blood and the Moon"), and Yeats is once again forced to accept the reality of the physical world.

Just as "Kubla Khan" has three principle divisions—the poet's interrupted dream described in the prose advertisement accompanying the poem, the Khan's vision of the pleasure dome, and the persona's failed vision at the end of the piece—I find three parallel divisions in the Byzantium poems. "Sailing to Byzantium" parallels the first two divisions of "Kubla Khan," while "Byzantium" parallels the third division. Specifically, in "Kubla Khan" the persona of the artist awakened by business pounding at the door strikes a similar chord in Yeats's opening lines of "Sailing to Byzantium." "That is no country for old men" is a waking statement. The persona is disturbed by the "dying generations." Where the one persona is not allowed his opiated rest, the other is not allowed to forget his age since "all neglect / Monuments of unageing intellect." Because "an aged man is but a paltry thing, / A tattered coat upon a stick," the persona leaps into the "desolate heaven" ("Nineteen Hundred and Nineteen") of his own imagination. He will sail "the seas and come / To the holy city of Byzantium." Coleridge's movement from opiate dreamscape to physical, real world is equivalent, though an inversion, to Yeats's movement from illusory, physical world to dreamscape's aesthetic reality.

The second phase begins here. The persona's declaration is parallel to the Khan's decree for the construction of his pleasure dome with "walls and towers . . . girdled round." We must remember this is *only* a decree. Voicing the declaration does not immediately construct the dome, for despite our godlike characteristics humanity cannot speak something immediately into physical existence. Rather, the dome is only an image in the Khan's imagination. Similarly, in "Sailing to Byzantium," the persona's declaration is what he wants and what he shall have only in his imagination as he had modeled previously in "The Lake Isle of Innisfree." When the persona states, "O sages standing in God's holy fire . . . gather me / Into the artifice of eternity," he has hit upon two essential concepts. First, God's fire is equal to the imaginative fires; if the one fire purges and purifies, so does the other. Secondly, eternity is artifice. If the Khan has his dome, Yeats has his dome in the aesthetic arch of his imagination. In some ways, this dome is equivalent to the battlements at the top of the tower: it separates the poet from the rest of humanity, which is located somewhere below him and occupied in base activities.

Ellmann states,

> The protagonist of the poem is not Yeats but may be described as a symbol of Yeats and of the artist and of man. . . . God in the

> poem stands less in the position of the Christian God than in that of supreme artist, artificer of eternity and the holy fire; he is thus also the poet and the human imagination which is sometimes in Yeats's system described as the maker of all things. (*Yeats* 254)

The persona, then, imagines he has found himself a perfect place in Byzantium because it is fabricated by the supreme artist. He seeks what Okifumi Komesu calls "the eternal image" (77). This is found in section IV, the last section of the poem:

> Once out of nature I shall never take
> My bodily form from any natural thing,
> But such a form as Grecian goldsmiths make
> Of hammered gold and gold enamelling. . . .

Giorgio Melchiori says that, here, "Nature is rejected, and the poet shows how faithful he has remained to the doctrine of art for art's sake current in his youth" (210). While this may be, Melchiori overlooks what transpires in the last four lines. The image of the bird does not belong to the "dying generations." As noted in Chapter One, the rhythmic change in the final four lines of the poem illustrates the problem of art for art's sake. The Khan's pleasure dome was intended to be a sanctuary against the outside world, just as the unnatural shape of the bird has nothing to do with the physical world. But the rhythm mirrors a change of attitude, a troubling of "animal blood" ("The Cat and the Moon"). First, the artist transformed into the shape of the bird is still neglected. The Emperor, who signifies God, is drowsy and, therefore, not listening intently. Which is worse? To be ignored by the dying generations or to be ignored by God? A greater dilemma is found in the last line. The bird sings of "what is past, or passing, or to come," but what do these matter if the song is sung in eternity where past, present, and future do not exist? "Ancestral voices" bring down the Khan's vision of the pleasure dome; Yeats's example illustrates how existence in his imaginative eternity is little, if at all, improved.

In "Kubla Khan," following the Khan's failed vision, the persona's vision in the final section also fails. He has had a vision, but he cannot "revive" the maid's "symphony and song," though clearly he wants to. If he were blessed with such power, he could "build that dome in air"; this would make him formidable to all other humans. Specifically, his vision would separate him from other mortals because the act of creation would make him god-like. Poetic sensibility is holy ground, and the average human cannot enter it. Yeats is acutely aware of this. In the tower of his aesthetic intelligence, he fabricates an entire city, creates his God and his God's temple, and discovers the impermanence of his eternal city.

At the end of "Sailing to Byzantium," the poet's vision fades along with the altered cadence. Then, in "Byzantium," the persona tries to revive and recreate the vision.

However, once we have left reality again for Byzantium, and "the unpurged images of day recede," we find "the Emperor's drunken soldiery are abed," incapable of muster. The persona is no longer "golden bird," here, but man since he belongs to the "unpurged images." Consequently,

> A starlit or a moonlit dome disdains
> All that man is,
> All mere complexities,
> The fury and the mire of human veins.

The image of the dome is unmistakable. This is, at the very least, allusively Coleridge's dome. Melchiori writes:

> He had gone back to the archetypal pattern of the dome which had been so prominent especially in romantic poetry. Miss Maud Bodkin has explored its significance from an essentially psychological point of view, along Jungian lines. Yeats was unconscious of these overtones of the dome image, but was fully aware of its importance in the poetry of Coleridge and Shelley. "Kubla Khan" is the highest and most open expression of a certain symbolic cluster which became nearly obsessive in the poems of the second romantic generation: the dome, the caves and the water. This cluster recurs in the poems of Shelley and Keats and its ascendency and influence has been examined by Wilson Knight who traces it back into Pope and Milton, and forward through Tennyson and Browning to Yeats. But Yeats in his early work, in spite of his avowed admiration for Shelley and of the obvious echoes of "Kubla Khan" in his poems, was fascinated by other symbols more closely related to his esoteric studies. In Shelley he preferred to see the poet-magician in his solitary tower, but eventually he realized that the poetry of symbolism, the only poetry he valued, was the poetry of "Kubla Khan." (226-27)

But the persona obviously does not belong to the eternal scene, here. The dome regards him contemptuously, along with all human complexities and passions. We do not find the poet as harmonious bird any longer; we find him outside the blessings of the eternal city. He is common and mortal, and part of "those dying generations" so clearly despised in "Sailing to Byzantium." Because of this awareness, what transpires afterwards is nightmarish and phantasmagorial.

The second stanza, for example, describes what Yeats terms the "superhuman," "death-in-life and life-in-death." The entity is "shade more than man, more image than a shade." It is death that may unwind death, death that may bring life:

> For Hades's bobbin bound in mummy-cloth
> May unwind the winding path;
> A mouth that has no moisture and no breath
> Breathless mouths may summon. . . .

Furthermore, the miracle of the golden bird first mentioned in "Sailing to Byzantium" is transformed in the third stanza of "Byzantium." "More miracle than bird or handiwork," it "can like the cocks of Hades crow, / Or, by the moon embittered, scorn aloud" "common bird or petal / And all complexities of mire or blood." Explicitly, while it is scorning these it is also scorning the untransformed persona. However, transformation is not impossible. Yeats describes in the fourth stanza an elaborate scene of god's purging fires:

> At midnight on the Emperor's pavement flit
> Flames that no faggot feeds, nor steel has lit,
> Nor storm disturbs, flames begotten of flame,
> Where all complexities of fury leave,
> Dying into a dance,
> An agony of trance,
> An agony of flame that cannot singe a sleeve.

The flames are purgatorial, and all those bodies of flesh, all those "complexities of fury," come to dance in it. Meanwhile, as we look into the last stanza, we see more bodies "astraddle on the dolphin's mire and blood, / Spirit after spirit!" to be purged in the eternal flames. "The smithies break the flood," Yeats writes. In other words, the bodies are transformed from the unpurged flesh of former selves to something alchemically new. The "marbles of the dancing floor," from which the fire arises, "break bitter furies of complexity," "those images that yet / Fresh images beget," and "that dolphin-torn, that gong-tormented sea." The fires purge all, not just flesh, but images belonging to the "Great Memory"—even the seas seem transformed. This purging is equivalent to the forgetfulness that occurs in myth when the Lethean waters are crossed.

Unpurged Yeats leaves us here, as unpurged as he is, riding those tormented seas because we have not gone through the transforming fires. Yeats cannot be the "golden bird" in the second poem because he cannot revive the original vision; considering the change of attitude found at the end of "Sailing to Byzantium," we must wonder if he would even desire the transformation into artifact. This, of course, does not deny the possibility of vision's return—the fires suggest that possibility. The metaphor of art, however, shows the intrusive world pulls him out of the vision. His subsequent efforts to return to the original dream create for him a nightmare. Good may come from that nightmare, but in the meantime he is locked "life-in-death, death-in-life." Even though the "dome" collapses for him because he stands apart from it, the architectural metaphor is the icon of the poet's self-knowledge and the vehicle by which the poet can reorder and recreate the structure of his real or imagined worlds. As "Byzantium" suggests, each time the imaginative process occurs, the aesthetic activity brings about unexpected, sometimes unwanted results; and, like the bodies astraddle the dolphins, even the old images become new in the imaginative, transforming fires.

As god himself, the creator-poet has knowledge of both internal and external worlds. This knowledge draws the poet nearer Unity of Being than he could ever otherwise hope. Without duality of vision, the poet could never hope for anything. In "Sailing to Byzantium," the poet elevates himself above the rest of humanity; humanity was somehow inferior. But once that vision is lost and he stands outside the eternal fires, he has become inferior to all those who come to be cleansed. As Yeats would write later in "The Circus Animals' Desertion," "Now that my ladder's gone / I must lie down where all the ladders start / In the foul rag and bone shop of the heart." Like his "stilted boys," he rose heroically above common humanity because his self-defining metaphor and his art-defining metaphor set him apart. In "Byzantium," he knows, as the Self knows, he must come to the fires of the holy city like everyone else, beyond vision, by living, by dying.

Chapter 6

The Metaphor of Dissolution: Ironic Vision in Yeats's Later Poems

Yeats once remarked, "I think profound philosophy must come from terror" (*Essays* 502). The remark chills: all philosophy, born from fear, attempts to shelter us from our terror, creates for us a masked reality, and provides a temporal sanctuary. Logic leaps: the stark reality that created terror first, and philosophy later, must still exist; if philosophy poses as reality, might it not create terror, too, and the proliferation of more *terrifying* philosophy? This is the very issue Yeats addresses in "Meru":

> Civilisation is hooped together, brought
> Under a rule, under the semblance of peace
> By manifold illusion; but man's life is thought,
> And he, despite his terror, cannot cease
> Ravening through century after century,
> Ravening, raging, and uprooting that he may come
> Into the desolation of reality: . . .

Here, then, is the irony of our existence. The "desolation of reality," what must be original terror—or its creator—is the very thing humanity quests after. Without illusion, our universe is not "hooped together." "Things fall apart," Yeats wrote in "The Second Coming"; "the centre" of our existence "cannot hold" unless we cling to tyrannical rule born from our terror.

Yeats's theme is a hard judgment. He has taken to task, in these few lines alone, all doctrine, all thought. What is reality? Rage and terror. This concept may make us uncomfortable, but Yeats does not intend to comfort us or himself. His task is to dissolve the old forms we live by to reveal the source of all forms.

He explains that intention well in "Are You Content?":

> I call on those that call me son,
> Grandson, or great-grandson,
> On uncles, aunts, great-uncles or great-aunts,
> To judge what I have done.
> Have I, that put it into words,
> Spoilt what old loins have sent?
> Eyes spiritualised by death can judge,
> I cannot, but I am not content.

By calling on his ancestry, Yeats purposes to link past to present. Nearing his own death, the aging poet wants to know if he has spoiled "what old loins have sent," those illusions he condemned in "Meru." The question must be directed at those who have died, for in a world where reality is masked, only "eyes spiritualised by death can judge." In death, and there only, unencumbered by swaying thought, can one's spirit know reality. Explicit in this poem, too, is that statement: "I am not content." But why is Yeats discontented? To find that answer, one might compare "Are You Content?" to "What Then?" In the latter poem, Yeats wrote, "The work is done"; in "Are You Content?" he called on the dead to "judge what I have done." As Arra Garab puts it, "Old age is not for satisfaction because ageless creative 'work,' forever hovering ghostlike, is never really 'done'" (56). Therefore, Yeats is not content that he has spoiled what he hoped to spoil. He has not fully "come" into the "desolation of reality."

One wonders if Wallace Stevens's comment that the poet's purpose "is to help people to live their lives" (30) is true for Yeats. In Yeats we have a poet who is dissatisfied, who seeks to spoil old values and to draw attention to the irony of our spirtitual and philosophical pursuits. Yeats, too, seems inconsistent in his own ideologies, and a student of Yeats must resolve those inconsistencies. Ellmann tells us that early in Yeats's career the poet hoped to be known as an Irish writer (*Identity* 4). During this period, Yeats used "the Romantic tradition of quest and vision" and coalesced it to "a national mythology" (Bloom 82). However, during Yeats's middle period, which Bloom incorrectly calls "so disappointing," Yeats's sentiments change. This change Bloom attributes to the "personal wreck" of Yeats's Romanticism (162). Yeats would next divert his attentions and energies toward a personal mythology—or philosophy. *A Vision* would captivate Yeats's attention for several years.

How, then, is it possible to find Stevens's purpose in a reading of Yeats? By most appearances, if we are to believe Ellmann and Bloom, it seems Yeats was unaware of his own poetic intentions. Likely, Ellmann's and, especially, Bloom's appraisals of early Yeats are erroneous, prejudiced as they are by their own critical preferences. But if we accept those appraisals, how can we justify the extremities of Yeats's subjects and themes? How can Yeats, posing as a philosopher, ridicule philosophy?

I think the answers to each of these questions can be found in Yeats's later poems. In those poems, Yeats's "thought which based itself on the insolubility of Kant's antinomies" illustrates "that the energy which drives the world comes from irreconcilable oppositions" (Clougherty 38). In those poems, Yeats's purposes as a poet are consistent with Stevens's. There, learning from Nietzsche the irony of philosophy, Yeats is no philosopher. A philosopher creates "manifold illusion"; Yeats, despite his own terror, chooses not to create a permanent world of artifice, as we see him attempt in "Sailing to Byzantium."

As Robert F. Garratt notes, what caused the change in Yeats's later poems may have been his abandonment of the Revival, a literary movement he helped create, if not invent, in favor of the Ascendancy tradition (19, 36). Garratt writes,

> Yeats's profound sadness and sense of personal failure forced him to recognize that his poetic attempts to deal with life were really maneuvers to avoid it. Or Yeats simply may have understood that as a poet he had moved as far as he could in one direction, that he had exhausted the life of his symbols, and that he needed to shift his poetic strategy. Whatever the cause, the poetry did begin to change after the turn of the century, gradually at first, but definitively, curbing excessive emotion with the emergence of a distinct sense of personality and a cultivation of the individual. (31)

Furthermore, Yeats's "mythologizing of the Protestant Ascendancy" provided him a means by which he could "measure the modern world and find it wanting" (Garratt 36). Rather than build upon the old themes of the Revival, of Irish nationalism, his later poems would envision the modern world in reductive terms; therein lies the strength of his later work.

Yeats's reductivism is central to a study of the later poems. It characterizes a prevalent rhetorical change in Yeats's poetry and is dominated by the metaphor of dissolution and by irony. The rhetorical change is notably important. Even in his earliest poems, Yeats asked questions. However, those questions were rarely as important as they would be later on. Compare, for example, lines from "The Song of the Happy Shepherd" to lines from "A Dialogue of Self and Soul." In the former, the question is stated in archaic poetic diction:

> Where are now the warring kings?
> An idle word is now their glory,

By the stammering schoolboy said,
Reading some entangled story:
The kings of the old time are dead; . . .

The syntax here, borrowed from high Victorian influences, is sprung excessively, seeming like awkward Tennyson or Arnold. An unintentional irony is found in "entangled story" and in "the kings of the old time are dead." The syntax of "The Song of the Happy Shepherd" is itself an "entangled story"; and just as "kings of the old time are dead," such poetry was "of the old time."

The diction and syntax of "A Dialogue of Self and Soul" differs greatly. For one thing, it is much more conversational, much more direct:

A living man is blind and drinks his drop.
What matter if the ditches are impure?
What matter if I live it all once more?
Endure that toil of growing up;
The ignominy of boyhood; the distress
Of boyhood changing into man;
The unfinished man and his pain
Brought face to face with his own clumsiness; . . .

Stylistically, "A Dialogue of Self and Soul" is much stronger than "The Song of the Happy Shepherd." By juxtaposing the two examples, one finds Yeats coming "face to face with his own clumsiness." Despite the differences in diction and poetic style, the rhetoric of the questions poses significant contrasts. Questions in Yeats's early poems, in stilted language, are directed toward Romantic notions; in "The Song of the Happy Shepherd," the question concerns itself with Irish legend and the death of mimetic tradition in art. In later poems, the questions are internalized and simultaneously more universal. I do not doubt that Yeats is asking these questions about his place in the "desolation of reality," transforming the poet from boy to man to "unfinished" old man in "A Dialogue of Self and Soul." In this poem, Yeats's irony is intended: "unfinished" not only means that his work is incomplete, it means he has not yet found unity of self and soul. Nor does he seek it any longer.

The multiplicity of Yeats's questions is more than a curiosity. In the early poem, only two questions were asked. "A Dialogue of Self and Soul," a poem of comparable length, yielded seven. The frequency indicates the importance of the poet's new themes: he tries to resolve the questions of his life and of the "desolation of reality." The comparison of question-frequency between these two poems is analogous to the frequency one would find in all early poems compared to those of Yeats's later period. The conclusion, then, is that Yeats felt a more insatiable need to search the soul later in his life. Consequently, the questions are going to be much more significant and their concerns not nearly so insular or specialized.

The *question* of *question* is certainly worth further study; however, of more central concern to the late poems is Yeats's use of irony and his invention of the metaphor of dissolution. While Yeats never terms this particular scheme the "metaphor of dissolution," he neared the terminology in a statement in 1938:

> According to Rilke a man's death is born with him and if his life is successful and he escapes mere "mass death" his nature is completed by its final union with it. In my own philosophy the sensuous image is changed from time to time at predestined moments called *Initiatory Moments* . . . . One sensuous image leads to another because they are never analyzed. At *The Critical Moment* they are dissolved by analysis and we enter by free will pure unified experience. When all the sensuous images are dissolved we meet true death.[1] (Wade 917)

While this particular statement was made at the end of Yeats's career, the metaphor is nonetheless a scheme with which Yeats began working at the end of his middle period. If we read "The Wild Swans at Coole," we read prime examples of "sensuous images" dissolved to "meet true death." How the metaphor of dissolution works is relatively simple. Yeats begins with externals:

> The trees are in their autumn beauty,
> The woodland paths are dry,
> Under the October twilight the water
> Mirrors a still sky;
> Upon the brimming water among the stones
> Are nine-and-fifty swans.

The details here belong to "initiatory moments"; at the end of the first stanza, Yeats creates the first in a series of "critical moments," narrows his focus to concrete specifics, dissolves the image, and internalizes it in the next stanza:

> The nineteenth autumn has come upon me
> Since I first made my count;
> I saw, before I had well finished,
> All suddenly mount
> And scatter wheeling in great broken rings
> Upon their clamorous wings.

The internalizing dissolves into the remembered image of the flight, and, at the "critical moment," the image of flight dissolves. Internalizing once more, Yeats discovers the significance of the experience. Despite the swans' static cycle, that they are "unwearied still," "all's changed" for the aging Yeats. He tells us, "Their hearts have not grown old; / Passion or conquest, wander where they will, / Attend upon them still." The terror he feels is found in the final lines:

> Among what rushes will they build,
> By what lake's edge or pool
> Delight men's eyes when I awake some day
> To find they have flown away?

Yeats discovers more than remorse here. The metaphor of dissolution completed, this is where Yeats meets "true death," an eternal nothingness posed against the delight of "men's eyes" who live still with the vision of the swans before them. The image of the swans is perpetual; they will fly eternally. However, the poet's image of himself is mutable; he cannot fly with the swans because his eyes have imprisoned him to earthly deterioration.

The metaphor of dissolution typically begins externally and turns inwardly, leaving the poet in the "desolation of reality." While Yeats used the metaphor in his early writing, he did not use it skillfully. This is due in part, perhaps, to the various thematic distractions of his earlier periods; artifice was simply not as important as it was later. It may be due to the poet's "immature" talents: he was neither capable nor knowledgeable enough of "desolation."[2] However, the metaphor of dissolution becomes necessary for the aging poet for two primary reasons. First, as Ellmann states, "As Yeats grew older his sense of life sharpened, and he dwelt more boldly upon its lust and rage, its mire and fury, but also envisaged more passionately the state of completeness to which incompleteness may attain" (*Modern Poetry* 110). The metaphor is Yeats's *modus operandi*; through it, he can find antithetical unity. When Yeats confronts life's "lust and rage, its mire and fury," he thrusts against passion and chaos the antinomies of love and solace, order and peace. Such juxtaposition results in a negating effect; the one cancels out the other, leaving us in what might be called *cosmic zero*. This does not suggest an emptying, for the antithetical ingredients exist dissolved in solution. Thus, if we want to live harmoniously, we must embrace both the burden and the joy of our existence. Secondly, the metaphor of dissolution provides Yeats with "self-transforming awareness" (Levine 10). Art transforms, and the reductive metaphor aids transformation. "The poem is made," Levine says, "to reflect the perfection that the poet wants to achieve, and so helps collapse the poet's ego" (14). Yeats wrote,

> The more a poet rids his verses of heterogeneous knowledge and irrelevant analysis, and purifies his mind with elaborate art, the more does the little ritual of his verse resemble the great ritual of Nature, and become mysterious and inscrutable. He becomes, as all the great mystics have believed, a vessel of the creative power of God. (*Essays* 201-02)

Readers of Yeats will not have much difficulty finding examples of the metaphor in the body of Yeats's work. While acknowledging its importance to such pieces as "Leda and the Swan" and "The Second Coming," it is used most in the poetry Yeats wrote about old age. As Garab tells us (quoting Yeats in part), " 'Denunciation of old age' is indeed a recurring and major motif, and its persistence is one of the most striking features of his poetry" (6). While certain scholars, such as Levine, call Yeats's poetry "the destructive vision" (102), the metaphor of dissolution is far more positive than the word *destructive* connotes. If profound philosophy arises from terror, we might suppose that what terrified Yeats most was old age. Consider, as example, two poems: "Death" and "Why Should Not Old Men be Mad?" In "Death," Yeats writes:

> Nor dread nor hope attend
> A dying animal;
> A man awaits his end
> Dreading and hoping all;
> Many times he died,
> Many times rose again.
> A great man in his pride
> Confronting murderous men
> Casts derision upon
> Supersession of breath;
> He knows death to the bone—
> Man has created death.

If "man awaits his end / Dreading and hoping all," and if he in his imagination has died "many times," then man must be obsessed with death. Surely, Yeats is obsessed: most of his poems deal specifically with aging and death (Levine 6). Here, too, Yeats looks sharply at philosophy when he writes, "Man has created death." Philosophy may try to shield us from terror, but it creates terror, too. If Yeats hopes, even in old age to be a "great man in his pride," he will confront "murderous men"—philosophers—fearlessly.

In "Why Should Not Old Men be Mad?" Yeats's fear justifiably turns into rage. As old men make "bad advance" toward age, "no single story would they find / Of an unbroken happy mind, / A finish worthy of the start." Take note, especially, of the irony in "unbroken happy mind." The "happy mind," for Yeats, must be broken; otherwise, spiritual unity cannot happen. Age, however, is clearly despised. Yeats also implies youth should be despised because "young men know nothing of this sort." "Observant old men," however, "know it well," and should be praised. But neglect, and knowledge of aging and of impending, unfair death, is "why an old man should be mad." At the poem's end, however, *mad* suggests more than anger; *madness* means *vision.*

Although Yeats may not resolve himself to the world's perception of aging, he must come to terms with its tragedy. The metaphor of dissolution provides Yeats this resolve. After all, philosophy does not bring solace. But the metaphor lets Yeats work through despair and fear actively. As Yeats said, "Passive suffering is not a theme for poetry. In all the great tragedies, tragedy is a joy to the man who dies . . ." (*Oxford* xxxiv-v). For Yeats to come through life heroically, he must find joy at the end of his metaphor.

"Nineteen Hundred and Nineteen," from early in Yeats's later period, shows aptly how the poet nears his ultimate, desolate joy:

> Many ingenious lovely things are gone
> That seemed sheer miracle to the multitude,
> Protected from the circle of the moon
> That pitches common things about. Here stood
> Amid the ornamental bronze and stone
> An ancient image made of olive wood—
> And gone are Phidias' famous ivories
> And all the golden grasshoppers and bees.

Yeats begins with all "ingenious lovely things": ornamentation, artifice, Greek culture and philosophy. All of these "are gone." In the second stanza, Yeats writes, "We too had many pretty toys when young." The ambiguity in *we* suggests not only *youth* but *Romantics* and their "toys." But these, too, are lost.

The tragedy of loss is found in the fourth stanza:

> Now days are dragon-ridden, the nightmare
> Rides upon sleep: a drunken soldiery
> Can leave the mother, murdered at her door,
> To crawl in her own blood, and go scot-free;
> The night can sweat with terror as before
> We pieced our thoughts into philosophy,
> And planned to bring the world under a rule,
> Who are but weasels fighting in a hole.

"Meru," written fifteen years later, would echo these sentiments. In "Nineteen Hundred and Nineteen," however, in that year's turbulence, philosophies become dragons, and this "nightmare / Rides upon sleep." Those who "planned to bring the world under a rule" are "weasels fighting" in the abyss of the world. In the midst of such chaos, the question asked in stanza six must *be*, "Is there any comfort to be found?" The answer, twenty years before Yeats's death, would surely seem to be, "No."

However, in section III, having turned the externals on himself, and as the previous imagery dissolves, the poet writes, "A man in his own secret meditation / Is lost amid the labyrinth that he has made / In art or politics." Once again, Yeats resurrects the swan symbol:

> The swan has leaped into the desolate heaven:
> That image can bring wildness, bring a rage
> To end all things, to end
> What my laborious life imagined, even
> The half-imagined, the half-written page; . . .

If the swan symbol is consistent with those found in "The Wild Swans of Coole" (and I am certain that it is), it is the manifestation of the poet's passions and imagination plunged "into the desolate heaven." All dreams, meant "to mend / Whatever mischief seemed / To afflict mankind," have come from collective lunacy: "we were crack-pated when we dreamed." If we read this particular line juxtaposed to the last line of "Why Should Not Old Men be Mad?" we find the word *mad* as an irony consistent to "crack-pated."

If Yeats's work has been "crack-pated," if Yeats has been fruitless, his comfort comes from self-mockery. In section V, Yeats invites his reader to "come let us mock at the great," "at the wise," "at the good"; "Mock mockers after that," Yeats writes, including himself in the satire. According to Bloom, the poem "renders all action mere murder, and he retreats into self-mockery" (356). This poem illustrates how the poet's "own system does not save, cannot comfort" (362).

Garab explains, however, that as "time and history took fire in [Yeats's] imagination, he came to discover the exhilarating joy of life sparked by the smart of tragic circumstance" (45). Therefore, part of joy comes from irony. Consider how the metaphor of dissolution and irony work together in "The Lamentation of the Old Pensioner"[3]:

> Although I shelter from rain
> Under a broken tree,

My chair was nearest to the fire
In every company
That talked of love or politics,
Ere Time transfigured me.

The juxtaposition of past and present is the metaphor of dissolution at "play," here. The persona, now an old man, has experienced the dissolution of his life; his body is the "broken tree" his soul finds shelter beneath. Metaphorically, *rain* may be life's turmoil, "manifold illusion" made concrete since the rules we live by exclude old people from "every company / That talked of love or politics." When the persona says his "chair was nearest to the fire," he refers to his youth, when he was a burning and eager participant in argument. Now, because he accepts the illusion, he implicitly accepts a different kind of fire, the one in the hearth that will keep his old bones warm. *Fire*, then, suggests the heat of argument in one instance and comfort in old age in the next. Clearly, the persona favors the former type of fire. For the poet, also an old man, the fire is inspiration: metaphorically, his "fire" is in his head.

But relentless Time has also "transfigured" Yeats. Used ironically, too, the word suggests both bodily corruption and spiritual perfection. If we attribute traditional symbolic values to the tree, it is a symbol of knowledge. "Broken" knowledge is the "desolation of reality" found in the antithetical union of bodily corruption and spiritual perfection. When Yeats writes, "I spit into the face of Time / That has transfigured me," he puts on his ironic mask in a show of defiance. However futile the act, there exists a potent joy in the pose. Garab explains that "the speaker has been devastated and reduced by time; yet time's workings have illumined his being and granted him heightened vision" (11-12).

Similarly, Yeats strives toward heroic vision in "Among School Children." According to Ellmann in *The Identity of Yeats*,

> Yeats speaks of the powerful theories of Plato, Aristotle, and Pythagoras, only to dismiss them because the theories, great as they were, proved powerless to avert the philosophers' own decrepitude and death. Power and knowledge . . . cannot exist together. Yet there is one escape from mortality: when our eyes are blinded by love, like those of a mother regarding her son, of a lover regarding his beloved, or of a nun regarding Christ, we see images which are independent of life or fact . . . . Because they do not depend upon observation, and in fact flout the evidence of the senses to which decay and mortality are real, they are 'self-born.' (229)

As in so many of Yeats's poems that begin with "initiatory moments," so too does “Among School Children”:

> I walk through the long schoolroom questioning;
> A kind old nun in a white hood replies;
> The children learn to cipher and to sing,
> To study reading-books and histories,
> To cut and sew, be neat in everything
> In the best modern way—the children’s eyes
> In momentary wonder stare upon
> A sixty-year-old smiling public man.

The mask Yeats wears as a “public man” establishes the irony of the entire poem. His thoughts, at the moment, are very private; only as the poem progresses, as his images dissolve, will he unveil the privacy to become “public.” Just as important, the “questioning” man is all too aware of the ironies around him. What the children are learning is actually the stuff of “manifold illusion.” Hence, “the best modern way” must be ironic. *Best* suggests *worst*, and *modern* is obviously archaic domestic training. Yeats is “smiling,” and this, too, is an ironic mask.

Once this “initiatory moment” has been dissolved, an image of a “Ledaean body” comes to Yeats’s mind. This image begins an “obsessive reverie of Maud Gonne” (Reid 184). He remembers “a tale that she / Told of a harsh reproof,” and that image blends with others: of Maud Gonne as a young, beautiful woman, and as an old crone, “Hollow of cheek as though it drank the wind / And took a mess of shadows for its meat.” The metaphor of dissolution leads Yeats from the tragedy of that image into a present image of himself:

> And I though never of Ledaean kind
> Had pretty plumage once—enough of that,
> Better to smile on all that smile, and show
> There is a comfortable kind of old scarecrow.

Momentarily, the tone becomes self-mocking. Yeats juxtaposes himself to the “daughters of the swan,” but checks his sarcasm quickly. “Better to smile on all that smile,” he says, leaving the children with an image of a “comfortable kind of old scarecrow.” While he may have dropped the sarcasm, he cannot completely drop the irony. His “heart driven wild,” he is anything but “comfortable.”

One cannot omit the sorrow the irony implies either. Age meets its antithesis in the schoolroom; one who decries philosophy is in the company of nuns; one who feels great passion has lost love. But as Ellmann explains, “Ecstasy comes from desperate sorrow” (*Identity* 230). The metaphor of dissolution has served its purpose, and Yeats arrives at pure image. Therefore, when Yeats invokes his perfected spirit—"O self-born mockers of man's enterprise"—it is the voice of a whole man that writes:

> Labour is blossoming or dancing where
> The body is not bruised to pleasure soul,
> Nor beauty born out of its own despair,
> Nor blear-eyed wisdom out of midnight oil.

Ellmann explains this exceptionally well: "For in life the body is bruised to pleasure soul, beauty comes only from despair at its lack, and wisdom is stained by the toil with which it is gained" (*Identity* 230). Reality, then, is no such enterprise. Because of this, Yeats concludes that the imagination which sees all things simultaneously and purely is the pervading emblem of salvation. For, as Edmund Wilson puts it, "What use is philosophy now?—is not all beauty bound up with the body and doomed to decay with it? is not even the divine beauty itself which is worshipped there by the nuns inseparable from the images of it they adore?" (62). The inseparable images allow Yeats to ask his final important questions:

> O chestnut-tree, great-rooted blossomer,
> Are you the leaf, the blossom or the bole?
> O body swayed to music, O brightening glance,
> How can we know the dancer from the dance?

When all is perfected, unified in the self-born imagination, and the "two natures" are "blent . . . Into the yolk and white of the one shell," image lets us see everything concurrently alive!

"Sailing to Byzantium" is thematically similar to "Among School Children." However, the tone is bitterly sarcastic. This is due in part to the neglect Yeats feels: "That is no country for old men." The younger, "dying generations," Yeats writes, are "caught in that sensual music" of youthful lust. As I have noted elsewhere, they ignore "monuments of unageing intellect." Yeats wears his ironic mask here: he sees himself as such a "monument," otherwise he would not have seen fit to take his imaginative journey. Additionally, his description of the youth as birds and fish is ironic: they are equally parts of what is born and dies.

When Yeats sails to the perfection of an imaginary landscape, represented here by Byzantium, he searches for himself "at the center of Unity of Being, a city where the spiritual life and the creation of art merge as one" (Bloom 345). Yeats calls this merger "the artifice of eternity." However, we must recognize the irony of the last stanza for reasons detailed in Chapter One and Chapter Five. The quest for aesthetic perfection is futility, too. Yeats is not "out of nature"; he "is where he always was, poised before his own artifact" (Bloom 347). We dare not overlook the lack of attention the poet feels even in the presence of a drowsy Emperor. Yeats no sooner builds his metaphorical Paradise than its image dissolves, along with its God, before his mind's eye.

If the poet cannot find complete contentment in artifice, then, what are the alternatives? We once again get the impression it must be in the "desolation of reality." As Yeats says in "A Dialogue of Self and Soul":

> I am content to live it all again
> And yet again, if it be life to pitch
> Into the frog-spawn of a blind man's ditch,
> A blind man battering blind men;
> Or into that most fecund ditch of all,
> The folly that man does
> Or must suffer, if he woos
> A proud woman not kindred of his soul.
>
> I am content to follow to its source
> Every event in action or in thought;
> Measure the lot; forgive myself the lot!
> When such as I cast out remorse
> So great a sweetness flows into the breast
> We must laugh and we must sing,
> We are blest by everything,
> Everything we look upon is blest.

The reader will recall Yeats's dissatisfaction in "Are You Content?" In "A Dialogue of Self and Soul," Yeats comes to terms with his existence. If he cannot live again, he is at least "content to live it all again" in his images. Some of these may be of "the frog-spawn of a blind man's ditch . . . Or into that most fecund ditch of all, / The folly" of men who loved Maud Gonnes. For his own folly, he has no remorse: he can forgive himself. Still, as Bloom notes, irony veils this poem, too: "Self offers . . . to divest itself of everything except the life it has lived, which it would live again . . . . Painful enough; more painful is what the [last] stanza describes, the involuntary acceptance by the finished man" (375). What Bloom refers to here is the irony in the word *must.* Not an affirmation of faith, it is a directive that Yeats has no choice but to follow. When the sweetness flows, one *must* laugh and sing.

Similarly, in "Vacillation," we see how "between extremities / Man runs his course." According to Bloom extremities negate, and "so more than divinity lies beyond our antinomies; experience itself does" (394). Despite Yeats's resolve and peace in "A Dialogue of Self and Soul," he vacillates momentarily in this poem. In "Vacillation," blessèd euphoria is shorter lived:

> My fiftieth year had come and gone,
> I sat, a solitary man,
> In a crowded London shop,
> An open book and empty cup
> On the marble table-top.
>
> While on the shop and street I gazed
> My body of a sudden blazed;
> And twenty minutes more or less
> It seemed, so great my happiness,
> That I was blessèd and could bless.

While the result here is similar to the one found in "A Dialogue of Self and Soul," "twenty minutes more or less" seems a meager duration of blessedness for a man who has searched so long for the "desolation of reality." What the poet will discover, however, is that the memory of the twenty minutes will be more valuable than the actual twenty minutes. Or, as Wallace Stevens put it in "Thirteen Ways of Looking at a Blackbird," "I do not know which to prefer,… The blackbird whistling / Or just after."

Still, in section V of "Vacillation," we find Yeats slipping into remorse:

> Things said or done long years ago,
> Or things I did not do or say
> But thought that I might say or do,
> Weigh me down, and not a day
> But something is recalled,
> My conscience or my vanity appalled.

This is nothing like the speaker in "A Dialogue of Self and Soul." Furthermore, in section VII we have a parody of a conversation between Heart and Soul. The Soul says, "Seek out reality, leave things that seem." But the Heart says, "What theme had Homer but original sin?" With the poet poised between two extremities, the Soul says to forget about philosophies; the Heart, however, drawing upon Greek culture and upon the Judeo-Christian view of sin, leaves us with what seems to be a hard, theological last word.

In the following section, Yeats writes,

I—though heart might find relief
Did I become a Christian man and choose for my belief
What seems most welcome in the tomb—play a predestined part.
Homer is my example and his unchristened heart.

Yeats cannot allow theology the last word because theology is "manifold illusion." He did not "become a Christian man," though such a choice would be "most welcome in the tomb." Instead, he ironically plays "a predestined part" with Homer as his "example and his unchristened heart." What is Homer's example? I imagine that Yeats intends to play the role of pagan, "blind bard." However, unlike Homer's physical blindness and Greek paganism, Yeats's blindness will be his refusal to accept the illusory doctrines of this world. As Yeats says in "A Dialogue of Self and Soul," he will "pitch into the frog-spawn of a blind man's ditch, / A blind man battering blind men." Ironically, though he does not accept theology, his blindness will "pitch" him into the mire of those who blindly and dogmatically live according to Christian doctrine. Nothing less than a prophet, the poet, one kind of blind man, "batters" the other "blind men" with his revelatory art to instruct humanity.

Ironically, then, religious people are "blind men" of another type. We might expect that Yeats will somehow illustrate through his verses how his blindness is a preferred way to live. Several of the "Crazy Jane" poems are likely extensions of Yeats's last word. The best examples of this are "Crazy Jane and the Bishop" and "Crazy Jane Talks with the Bishop." Crazy Jane, an ironic mask, assaults religious figures with verbal pleasure. On the other hand, the Bishop, a symbol of theological dogma, patronizes. In "Crazy Jane and the Bishop," Crazy Jane interrupts the Bishop's speech repeatedly with "All find safety in the tomb." The remark is obviously anti-Christian. Because the Bishop cannot persuade Crazy Jane, the word *solid* is ironic. The Bishop, a "solid man," is weak compared to Crazy Jane; his theology is impotent against the "desolation of reality."

In "Crazy Jane Talks with the Bishop," Crazy Jane tells him that "fair and foul are near of kin, / And fair needs foul." The antithesis should collapse into one solution: the Bishop hopes to build God's kingdom; Crazy Jane makes it dissolve. According to the plan of the metaphor of dissolution, the negation of extremities should produce joy; we cannot discover Unity of Being if we live our lives in extremity. When the metaphor of dissolution dissolves the extremities into one solution, we discover more nearly "full humanity" (Bloom 441). Consequently, the solution is revealed in the last four lines:

Love has pitched his mansion in
The place of excrement;
For nothing can be sole or whole
That has not been rent.

Although the Bishop's self-righteousness destroys what he hopes to build, Crazy Jane's position is real, nearly Christian. The Bishop has lost sight of his evangelical purpose; his condemnation of Crazy Jane's "flat and fallen" breasts and her "foul sty" of a home cannot convert her. Condemnation is not evangelism; however, love is. Christianity was never meant to be exclusive, a point Crazy Jane knows intuitively. As Christ walked among the lepers, healed the diseased, ate with whores, and drank wine with drunkards, "Love had pitched his mansion in / The place of excrement." As Christ died to become holy God, "nothing can be sole or whole / That has not been rent." Extended metaphorically, Yeats, an unwhole old man, finds unified joy in the tragedy of his life, as Jane does. His place in the universe is a holy one; though "unwhole" in the eyes of the world, though old, he is more complete and more alive than those trapped in their illusory lives.

"Ribh Considers Christian Love Insufficient" is a similar poem:

> I study hatred with great diligence,
> For that's a passion in my own control,
> A sort of besom that can clear the soul
> Of everything that is not mind or sense.
> Why do I hate man, woman or event?
> That is a light my jealous soul has sent.
> From terror and deception freed it can
> Discover impurities, can show at last
> How soul may walk when all such things are past,
> How soul could walk before such things began.

Here, Yeats addresses "a major confrontation and justification of his own hatred" (Hasset 108). Ironically, the negative virtue of hate has positive results because "hatred of God may bring the soul to God." Enlightenment is found in dark jealousy, freeing the soul from "terror and deception." Once the soul is freed, it survives in the absence of all philosophy and nears godly perfection. "How soul may walk when all things are past, / How soul could walk before such things began" is illustrated elsewhere, too.

In "Lapis Lazuli," Yeats writes, "All things fall and are built again, / And those that build them again are gay." Whereas the "Ribh" poem calls for the destruction of the "impurities" of Christian love, "Lapis Lazuli" concentrates on creation, "the building again that follows a fall" (Hassett 148). Reconstruction is essential to the metaphor of dissolution; once all old forms have been dissolved, a spiritual rebuilding is necessary.

However, "Lapis Lazuli" poses certain difficulties, too. Bloom, apparently expecting some explicit moral prescription, is especially intolerant of the poem because "inhumane nonsense is not always the best foundation for aesthetic judgment, and perhaps we might be a little wary of 'the message of affirmation' Yeats is bringing to us" (438). He also takes to task certain of the allusions. For example, Bloom tells us, "The gaiety of Lear is of course non-existent" (439). My reading of the poem is not nearly so harsh. "Lapis Lazuli" is a particularly subtle posturing of the poet behind irony. When Yeats writes that "hysterical women say / They are sick of the palette and fiddle-bow, / Of poets that are always gay," Yeats nears comedy in self-mockery. The persona of the poem casts himself into the group of "gay" poets. We have seen other examples where Yeats is obsessed with human tragedy. However, is that "gay"? Somehow, the poet must transform the tragedy into joy. Somehow, gaiety must transfigure all that dread. When he describes "tragic *play*" (emphasis added), how "there struts Hamlet, there is Lear, . . . They know that Hamlet and Lear are gay," Yeats is playing with irony. The word *struts* is ludicrous. Hamlet, who says, "O that this too too solid flesh would melt, / Thaw, and resolve itself into a dew" hardly struts. He wants to dissolve. Hamlet's boldest actions come from his "antic disposition," an act he puts on. For the knowledgeable audience, his actions are not confusing but humorous. Yeats may introduce tragedy, but the comic proportions are not intended to be wisdom. They are simply the means by which we may transcend the tragic to find joy. We might mock the tragic; we might rebuild upon the ruins of our world; we might listen to music; or we may act out a silly part; in each case, we find gaiety though the tragic is omnipresent. If we feel too much of the world's tragedy, we could not live. Thus, because this poem addresses a serious subject in less than serious terms, "Lapis Lazuli" is clearly a muted mad song.

We can find a similar mad joy in "The Apparitions" and "The Wild Old Wicked Man." "There is safety in derision," Yeats writes in "The Apparitions." Obviously, the derisive voice is Yeats's. He ridicules himself, if not everything philosophical. When he says that the worst appartition he has seen is "a coat upon a coat-hanger," we can take the comment literally: the too-serious man has no soul; he is as empty as that coat. However, since the word *derision* anchors the end of the first line, we might suspect that Yeats once again poses behind irony, this time sarcasm. In the second stanza, he writes:

> I have found nothing half so good
> As my long-planned half solitude
> Where I can sit up half the night
> With some friend that has the wit
> Not to allow his looks to tell
> When I am unintelligible.

Notice the repetition of the word *half.* Except for the long-planning, everything else is in halves. As for wits, only one person has whole wit: the guest. By inference alone, self-mockery leads us to believe Yeats speaks of his own half-wittedness when he writes of his being "unintelligible." But, in this manner, "a man grows old" and "his joy / Grows more deep day after day." Bloom describes it as

> Yeats's own heroic humanism, . . . a growing natural joy, filling the depths of the empty heart. It is a joy of natural knowledge, purchased at the cost of power, unlike antithetical joy, but purchased at a good price. The knowledge is a finding of limited good, of a strength allowing mystery to be faced without mystification, and fright without mythology. As knowledge, it is skeptical even of skepticism. (455)

But where does this "natural joy" take us? Where does it take Yeats? It leads into the pit of terror with which Yeats was so obsessed. Yet we enter that "desolation of reality" unafraid. In "The Gyres," for instance, Yeats thrusts us back into profound philosophy and its results:

> Things thought too long can be no longer thought,
> For beauty dies of beauty, worth of worth,
> And ancient lineaments are blotted out.
> Irrational streams of blood are staining earth;
> Empedocles has thrown all things about;
> Hector is dead and there's a light in Troy;
> We that look on but laugh in tragic joy.

The first stanza calls to mind images similar to the "blood-dimmed tide" of "The Second Coming." In "The Gyres," however, in the midst of "mere anarchy," there is laughter and joy. The poet says, "Rejoice!" and "What matter?" For, as Henn states in *The Lonely Tower*, "There will be a new civilization, a new aristocracy, to take the place of the old" (320). Yeats wrote,

> As we approach the phoenix nest the old classes, with their power of co-ordinating events, evaporate, the mere multitude is everywhere with its empty photographic eyes. Yet we who have hated the age are joyous and happy. The new discipline whenever enforced or thought will recall forgotten beautiful faces . . . . (*Essays* 320-21)

The last line of the poem, "all things run / On that unfashionable gyre again," contains a wonderful ambiguity. "Unfashionable gyre," as I have said in Chapter Four, unifies this later poem with *A Vision* and "The Second Coming." However, *unfashionable* not only means "untrendy" and "unpopular," it is more of Yeats's self-mockery: his system was inadequate; he could not fashion it beyond its intangibility. Once the metaphor of dissolution completes its work, Yeats can acknowledge his failure. That acknowledgment is cause for joy because it comes from self-transformation.

Other poems show equally well the reductive metaphor, the irony, and the self-derision. However, the most important poem from this period is "The Circus Animals' Desertion." Initially, the poem seems despairing:

> I sought a theme and sought for it in vain,
> I sought it daily for six weeks or so.
> Maybe at last, being but a broken man,
> I must be satisfied with my heart, . . .

Searching for new themes is futile. Bradford suggests that Yeats fears "he is too old to find one" (157). However, we have seen reference to brokenness before, in "The Lamentation of the Old Pensioner" and in the figure of the poet as a paltry thing in "Sailing to Byzantium." I suspect Yeats is staging a final pose, ironically admitting to the metaphor of dissolution as it affects his life and his art. But, as before, dissolution does not end with complete dissolve. Something else, a unification, takes place.

The line, "I must be satisfied with my heart," brings to mind certain of Yeats's earliest Romantic poems; however, this heart is different. It is experienced. Furthermore, if irony and metaphor work as Yeats had hoped, the heart now knows solace. Yeats's task is to unify troubled self with the peaceful heart. In part, this unity must come from self-evaluation; he must analyze what he had done: "My circus animals were all on show, / Those stilted boys, that burnished chariot, / Lion and woman and the Lord knows what." The "circus animals," his "body of motifs and symbols" (Rosenthal 222), are conspicuously absent (Bradford 157). Yeats alludes to a number of figures in those last two lines. According to Jeffares, "stitled boys" refers to Celtic legendary heroes and "Irish kings for whom nobody cared a farthing" (508). "Lion and woman" refers to Yeats's "Against Unworthy Praise," a poem about Maud Gonne (Jeffares 509). But the final words of this stanza are most important because they express Yeats's new attitude toward his old themes. "Lord knows what" is ironic because it first suggests that Yeats is amazed by his accomplishments; however, it also suggests his indifference toward his writing. Detached from the early figures, he understands they are of little use to him in his old age.

Yeats's criticism of his past continues in the second section of the poem. He recalls "how his personal needs and desires engendered the memorable themes of his earlier years" (Garab 56). However, implicit in that section is

Yeats's awareness that he can "but enumerate old themes." Because these came from "the embittered heart," Yeats must find a new theme-source. Divested of his images and his masks, he moves toward unity:

> Those masterful images because complete
> Grew in pure mind, but out of what began?
> A mound of refuse or the sweepings of a street,
> Old kettles, old bottles, and a broken can,
> Old iron, old bones, old rags, that raving slut
> Who keeps the till. Now that my ladder's gone,
> I must lie down where all the ladders start,
> In the foul rag-and-bone shop of the heart.

The "masterful images," grown out of a "pure mind," have deserted Yeats, but the desertion occurs because their purpose is completed. Complete image begets complete mind. This enables Yeats to evaluate his work, exposing the "disreputable origins" of his images (Rajan 182).

Yeats is resolved to "lie down where all the ladders start," believing he will find a natural bonding to the "old kettles, old bottles," "old iron, old bones, old rags." New poetic energy will come from the "disorderly profusion" of ideas (Mulryne 140). His Muse, appropriately, will be the "raving slut who keeps the till." Positioning himself lower than the ladder's bottom rung, Yeats is part of the world unformed. To use Garab's term once again, "heightened vision" in a lowly position is poetic unification of polarities.

But it is irony and the metaphor of dissolution that moves Yeats to this resolution. "The Circus Animals' Desertion" completes the process that Yeats had been working toward the last half of his life. In the "desolation of reality," Yeats finds he can strip off his masks and divest himself of all myths. There, an energy and a joy exist. There, to borrow from "Under Ben Bulben," "heavens had opened."

Chapter 7

High Talk: An Epilogue

The metaphors in Yeats's poetry provide him the single means by which he can most effectively present his vision of real and imagined worlds. "Words alone are certain good," as Yeats tells us in "The Song of the Happy Shepherd." We must be aware, however, of the reflexiveness of language. Words not only create the exacting power of metaphor but derive a good portion of their authority from metaphor. Words *mean*, but how words mean depends upon the metaphorical equivalences we appoint to words and the things they signify. In Yeats's example, much of the "good" in words (and, by extension, the power in his poems) depends upon the metaphors he fashions from words. Yeats's attentiveness to craft, which includes his careful selection and combination of forms, rhythm, and the subtleties of language, creates not an accidental magic nor a sleight of hand, a quick, creative wave which produces a bouquet of words; it creates, instead, a premeditated, purposeful sorcery. Yeats draws his readers into the poems, and he mesmerizes or entrances them by his evocative manipulation of poetic invention, including, most certainly, metaphorical strategies. He leads his readers to what seems prophetic, human truth.

For Yeats, the sources of the poem are always the unexplored, unsettled, or still untamed region that the poem tries to order. Even in poems which seem to repeat his existential concepts, Yeats actually pushes farther into the uncharted territory of those concepts. The notion of the poem, its inceptive impulse, "troubles [Yeats's] animal blood" ("The Cat and the Moon") so violently or supernaturally that he cannot help but "stalk on, stalk on" ("High Talk") in pursuit of the articulation that might bring him peace. When Yeats explores uncharted poetic territory, he encounters the task of appropriate and acute identification, clarification, elaboration, and signification of that territory.

Metaphor, in its diversity, is the consistent means by which he can accomplish this task; it is how he may create a dimensional representation that will excite and inform both himself and his readers.

The powerful complexity of Yeats's poetry defies singular theoretical classification or definition. This is why metaphor is so important to Yeats's work and to a understanding of Yeats's poetry. Metaphor is not an exclusive agent; it incorporates virtually all poetic techniques. As an interpretive tool, it embraces nearly all critical theories and helps to illuminate a poem where some specific theory may fail. If for no other reason than this, Yeats, surely, secures a permanent place for his poems because his metaphors attend to all aesthetic possibilities. He is not just a master of a single poetic scheme or concept, he is master of them all; consequently, he remains the "top cat" among modern poets.

Perhaps an effective illustration for what I have been discussing throughout these chapters is Yeats's "High Talk." Neither one of Yeats's most anthologized poems nor one of his most skillful, especially when compared to the more perfect "Leda and the Swan" or "The Wild Swans at Coole," "High Talk" is a risk-filled poem. It charts out, fairly methodically, the territory of his poetic career; it is Yeats's personal summation of who he is, what his place in the world is, and what he has endeavored to do throughout the body of his poetry. Simultaneously, the metaphorical inventiveness of the poem transforms its familiar territory into something miraculously new. It finds Yeats, toward the end of his life, reflecting upon his work with innovative genius and mad-joy. "High Talk" is Yeats at his most playful, his most self-effacing, his most defiant. Furthermore, the poem attests to the many metaphorical points I have discussed throughout these chapters.

I agree reservedly with B. L. Reid who writes,

> One hardly knows where to begin. It is a highly excited and deeply exciting poem. "All metaphor, Malachi, stilts and all." Yeats seldom stays with any metaphor so long as he stays with this one. That he develops this one so intricately, so long and grandly, in such mad speech, suggests that it satisfied him rarely and specially. (241)

Indeed, the poem commands notice because it is so excited, so very energetic. However, Reid's claim that Yeats usually failed to sustain metaphor for any length of time seems to belong to a school that perceives metaphor as a brief syntactical utterance of comparison, or that metaphor may extend only as far as analogy. As illustrated throughout these chapters, metaphor may be an utterance of any duration, quite broad in its conceptual applications, and quite significant to the shaping of a body of poetry. Metaphor lets the poet scrutinize the abstract and rediscover symbols and images previously buried in the "Great Memory." In Yeats's example, the abstract thing may be the insatiable desire to leave this physical world; it may be fear of old age and death; it may be despair and anger over forthcoming ruin; it may be passion; and it may entail far more than any of these concepts. The poet's obligation, if the verse is to breathe life into both poet and poet's audience, is to make the metaphorical concepts understood. Aesthetic understanding comes not just through concrete language and imagery, but through repetitions and patterns with which our collective consciousness can identify. This does not suggest merely a study in theme because metaphor may reveal theme. Metaphor is not peripheral to the study of literature; it is, first of all, the "highest" pursuit of the poet. "High Talk" illustrates that point as I have hoped to illustrate it in these previous chapters.

Secondly, very nearly everything valuable in a poem may be clarified by metaphorical scrutiny. In "The Cold Heaven," Yeats wrote the line, "Riddled with light." This is a fine point to make about metaphor. A poem is an intricate word-puzzle or riddle through which meaning is revealed by our attentive play; we pick out a piece of the puzzle, here or there, through symbol, prosody, rhythm, rhyme, language, until we have quite literally "riddled" the work with many interpretive holes. Ironically, the poetic puzzle is the one puzzle we get a clearer picture of when we dismantle it. The activity of "dissection," as Wordsworth would have called it, helps us to understand the poem better. However, if we undertake our interpretive activity with metaphor as our principal tool, I believe our work might not be so piecemeal. It might actually intensify the joy of solution.

Similarly, virtually everything in "High Talk" is significant; little can be dismissed, and much of it can be examined within the metaphorical concepts I have discussed previously. Yeats begins "High Talk" by comparing the act of poetry to a circus parade, as in "The Circus Animals' Desertion." He writes, "Processions that lack high stilts have nothing that catches the eye." What are processions to the poet but poems? Poems are the poet's parade and show. If the poet wants an attentive audience, the procession must have "high stilts"—high ideals, high imagination, and, with these, the high vision of imagery, symbol, and metaphor. The precarious height at which the poet marches separates the poet and the poetry from the "common herd" ("Cuchulain Fights with the Sea"). As discussed in Chapter Two, the poet seeks out alternative, aesthetic realities. This is serious business, surely. Here, however, the aesthetic reality is not that longed for island in the imagination; it is not the protective walls of the tower, as discussed in Chapter Five. The aesthetic reality is the self-elevated poet, balanced laughably upon stilts for the pleasure of both himself and his readers. Though the act of writing poetry may be a serious matter, it may result in giddy pleasure. The poetic impulse is a matter of need, certainly; poets have to write because they have to write. However, poets likely also enjoy the task of writing; they likely hope the audience will find pleasure in the poetic performance. Humanity may care very little to view its own commonness, a problem, perhaps, existent in realism. The common subject lacks freshness and vitality; it mirrors humanity's ordinariness and mediocrity. It may only intensify the bleak seriousness of existence. The metaphor, however, is both a pleasant distortion of reality and a new reality, just as poet as stilt-walker and poem as circus parade are simultaneously distortions and accurate descriptions. The distortion becomes the spectacle and the exotic. Common humanity may revel upon the fundamentally ludicrous act of stilt-walking because it somehow elevates them from their own mundanity.

Third, metaphor is analogous to the creative act of God. It defines who we are and the configuration of our system of beliefs; the metaphor speaks into existence our personal identities and our universes. Consider, again, "High Talk." The poet as stilt-walker asks,

> What if my great-granddad had a pair that were twenty foot high,
> And mine were but fifteen foot, no modern stalks upon higher,
> Some rogue of the world stole them to patch up a fence or a fire, . . .

Yeats uses the "stilt" metaphor to suggest several things. First, it may suggest a distinction between historical points, between past and present. "Great-granddad" may refer to Yeats's Irish heritage, perhaps allude to certain of his poems about Irish heroes. This seems obvious enough. However, "great-granddad" upon higher stilts brings also to mind poetic geneology. Yeats is a reluctant Modernist, though he identifies himself as one of the "last romantics" ("Coole Park and Ballylee, 1931"). Four generations extend backward from Yeats's place: from the Modern to the Victorian, and then from the second generation of the Romantics to the first generation (son, father, grandfather, great-grandfather). For the allusive pleasure of it, we might imagine Yeats's "great-granddad" is William Blake. In *A Vision*, Blake occupies a higher position than Yeats upon the configuration of the Great Wheel. Thus, Blake's stilts may be "twenty foot high" while Yeats's are fifteen.[1] Daniel Albright notes that "the stilts keep shrinking" because "the highest symbolic poetry is impossible in this stage of the historical gyre" (179). However, as Kermode explains, "[I]t should be remembered that the 15th Phase is a point at which the doctrines of isolation and Image come together in the system" (60). The poet upon his stilts occupies isolated space while all around him moves the procession of his poetic images.

Poet and poetic subject belong to the same metaphorical parade; they cannot be separated because one derives its definition or identity from the other. As Albright puts it, "The metaphoric tenor becomes lost in the metaphoric vehicle" (179). The two parts of metaphor collapse into each other, the stilts shorten, and the self-effacing poet, though heads above the rest of the Modern generation, walks on stilts shorter than certain poets of the past. Thus "High Talk's" metaphor, like metaphor in general, says something about who the poet is, by virtue of cultural and literary heritage, and by the configuration of a system of beliefs.

Furthermore, the metaphor defines for us what it is we desire and, subsequently, how we expect to fulfill our desire. The shortening of the poet's stilts directly opposes what the poet desires. This shortening may have resulted, in part, from the modern world's changing aesthetic tastes or needs. Granted, we need art, for reasons suggested in Chapter Four; we still desire the procession. However, "some rogue of the world" may want to make art practical and, perhaps, disposable. Hence, the rogue steals the stilts to build a fire or mend a fence. Yeats alludes, very subtly, to that intrusive world which brings him off his golden bough in "Sailing to Byzantium." The utility the rogue gives a poem may not coincide with the poet's purposes. The rogue's fire may not be the purging fires of "Byzantium"; it may be a destructive, anti-aesthetic fire.[2] What happens when the poet finds the stilts are gone? What does the poet do when it seems as if art would perish in those anti-aesthetic fires? In Yeats's case, the poet starts at ground-level, "where all ladders start" ("The Circus Animals' Desertion"). When the world's aesthetic values change, the poet comes down to earth, though temporarily. Starting out at ground-level places the poet upon the same turf as "the rogue." However, the intelligent poet does not languish there; the poet makes use of the opportunity to rise to defiant, new heights.

Granted, a poet might make use of the materials at ground-level, but "piebald ponies, led bears, caged lions, make but poor shows." Alluding to "The Circus Animals' Desertion," this menagerie may be representative of a poet's images and emblems, yet, because they are tamed and broken to domestic rule, they are insufficient in themselves to make a poem successful. There must be more,

> Because children demand Daddy-long-legs upon his timber toes,
> Because women in the upper stories demand a face at the pane
> That patching old heels they may shriek, . . .

Therefore, the poet writes, "I take to chisel and plane" in order to build another set of stilts. The poet's desire is not one easily satisfied. Poetry could not last if the poet accepted the loss of stilts; the inherent commonality of life would subdue and strangle the art. What the poet does, then, is fashion a new apparatus, a new set of legs; out of an act of stubborn will, the poet creates what will both elevate the author and the audience as the metaphorical distortion pleases and excites the crowd. Metaphor is a perfect tool: it guarantees infinite creation and recreation. Metaphorical combinations are countless, and, when a poet alights upon an ecstatic pairing, when the incongruity is such that it simultaneously clarifies while it challenges us by its unfamiliarity, we cannot help but feel the thrill that children feel or the silly, harmless panic of shrieking women.[3]

Metaphor, perhaps, is a remedy for an ailing civilization. If we can create and recreate endlessly because of metaphor on an aesthetic and poetic level, in microcosm, perhaps we can create and recreate through metaphor on a universal level, in macrocosm. In "Lapis Lazuli," Yeats wrote,

> I have heard that hysterical women say
> They are sick of the palette and the fiddle-bow,
> Of poets that are always gay,
> For everybody knows or else should know
> That if nothing drastic is done
> Aeroplane and Zeppelin will come out,
> Pitch like King Billy bomb-balls in
> Until the town lie beaten flat.

To suppose that art may be a vessel for our cure is drastic, certainly. Yet plausibility of the notion is as intriguing as the equivalence of poet to stilt-walker. If the poet elevates art, the poet might also elevate humanity above its destructive course. The poet's metaphors may create a new vision of humanity, a new esteem worth saving.

When the women shriek at the "face at the pane" in "High Talk," it is as much the poet's face as it is their own mirrored reflection.[4] It is, as well, the face of all humanity, distorted out of its current ordinariness. Located in the "upper stories," satirically bringing to mind the architectural and tower metaphors discussed in Chapter Five, the poet's intruding presence draws them pleasantly from their mundane labors. Significantly, the reference to taking "to chisel and plane" follows the women's work. Metapoetically, the line suggests aesthetic similarity to the "stitching and unstitching" found in "Adam's Curse." However, the medium and the tools have changed since Yeats gave up poetry's embroidery to "walk naked" ("A Coat"). The chisel is used in sculpture (bringing to mind "The Statues"), and the plane is a carpenter's tool used to smooth rough wood.[5] The new tools fashion both art and stilts, and the work is apparently more physical, the medium harder, than it has been in the past. Contrasted to the "patching [of] old heels," the stilt-walker's work, from the fashioning of the stilts to the poet's precarious balance upon them, is far more laborious, far more dangerous. This suggests, perhaps, the poet must concentrate, deliberate, and agonize more rigorously upon the difficulty of his craft.

It may seem, then, that nearly everything is metaphor or governed by metaphor, from the poet's own interpretation of self and world to, perhaps, the yoke we must bear if we expect to save ourselves and the world. Derrida tells us that "[There] is no nonmetaphoric language" (67). I wonder, now that this study is completed, if there is "no nonmetaphoric" reality. Often, while I read Yeats's poems, I was struck by how there cannot be any knowing of this world, or of this sometimes self-searching scholar, except through metaphorical perception.

I have begun to feel as Yeats feels at the conclusion of "High Talk." Yeats writes,

> Malachi Stilt-Jack am I, whatever I learned has run wild,
> From collar to collar, from stilt to stilt, from father to child.
>
> All metaphor, Malachi, stilts and all. A barnacle goose
> Far up in the stretches of night; night splits and the dawn breaks loose;
> I through the terrible novelty of light, stalk on, stalk on;
> Those great sea-horses bare their teeth and laugh at the dawn.

Who is Malachi? At this writing, because "whatever I learned has run wild" through these pages, Malachi is partly me, the one who wanted to learn something about metaphor, about Yeats's poetry, and about the writing of poetry. And, more obviously, Malachi, at the very least, is the persona of the poem. We can accept that literally enough. However, Malachi is multiply allusive. Finneran, in his edition of *The Poems of W. B. Yeats*, points out one Malachi from the many who seems pertinent to Yeats's metapoetics (679).[6] While each of Finneran's examples seem conceivable, the Biblical Malachi is especially worth noting. Malachi is the "messenger," just as Malachi Stilt-Jack utters "High Talk" to explain to us something about the writing of poetry. Compare Malachi's message, "[W]hatever I learned has run wild," to how Yeats's "heart was driven wild" in "Among School Children." If these are parallel, the heart is equal to what is learned. Poetry is the heart or soul of the poet bared to the world. Perhaps the next line supports this assertion. "From collar to collar" brings to mind "A Coat's" "there's more enterprise in walking naked" and Yeats's derision of old age in "The Apparitions" ("Fifteen apparitions have I seen; / The worst a coat upon a coat-hanger"). The poet leaves apparel's collar to wear the yoke of increased burden which Fergus wears. "[S]tilt to stilt" suggests not just Yeats's poetic parentage or the configuration of the Great Wheel but the necessity of coming down from the heights—to "fifteen foot"—to fashion new stilts or designs for poetry, in order to edify the human race.

In "Nineteen Hundred and Nineteen," Yeats wrote that "the swan has leaped into the desolate heaven." A metaphor for the poetic impulse, the swan cleaves through the darkness of the poet's mind and soul and lets in revelatory light. Now, in "High Talk," the poet has become the "barnacle goose," flying "in the stretches of night" where "night splits and the dawn breaks loose." The poet, no longer just a stilt-walker, is equivalent to the poetic impulse in his new incarnation; because of this equivalence, we cannot readily distinguish between the two as each component of the metaphor depends upon the other's significance. Consequently, the poet, "through the terrible novelty of light," will "stalk on, stalk on" the epiphanies metaphors reveal. In some respects, the poet is a configuration of the "rough beast," stalking poetic prey in the Bethlehem of aesthetic intelligence. Each step, each poem makes the poet less "rough." Consider, too, the similarity between "terrible novelty of light" and "a terrible beauty is born" ("Easter 1916"). The latter exemplifies tragic joy, how violence may create beauty; similarly, poetic inspiration is both terrible and beautifully revealing. Yeats, perhaps, has illustrated this antinomy better than any modern poet.

Finally, the "great sea-horses" refers both to the "horses of the sea" in "Cuchulain's Fight with the Sea" and to the dolphins of "Byzantium." In "Byzantium," the spirits cross into the eternal city on the backs of the dolphins; metaphorically, they are sea-horses. Furthermore, these sea-horses "bare their teeth and laugh at the dawn." The baring of teeth recalls the poet's defiant sneering: "I spit into the face of Time / That has transfigured me" ("The Lamentation of the Old Pensioner"). The laughter brings to mind "we that look on but laugh in tragic joy" ("The Gyres") and "gaiety transfiguring all that dread" ("Lapis Lazuli"). We might assume the sea-horses deride death's darkness while they simultaneously express joy at the prospect of eternity. However, derisiveness is directed at the dawn, in defiance of whatever the ensuing, eternal light may bring. Death, to the common beast, is comfort. Yeats wrote, "Nor dread nor hope attend / A dying animal" ("Death"). However, acceptance of life is defiant acceptance of the horror light may reveal. The poet, like Cuchulain, fights the "invulnerable tide" of the light, creating something beautiful and vital from its horrifying aspects.

"All metaphor, Malachi, stilts and all" is the summation of a life's work. *All* is metaphor. Malachi, the stilts, everything in the poetic procession, *is* metaphor. J. R. Mulryne says that "Yeats casts himself as Malachi Stilt-Jack, the maker of metaphors, of art in the grand manner. . . .[T]he activity he is committed to is a precarious one, carried out unnaturally, under strain" (140).[7] Perhaps this is correct in part: Yeats wrote poems in a "grand manner," but he was not fearful of writing poems in the ridiculous manner, either. The activity of art encompasses the artist; the two entwine and become inseparable. Still, as I indicated previously, the serious activity may be a joyful, silly, hilarious one. Yeats, the mature poet, understands how these antinomies are resolved and how this resolution may work in the writing of poetry. In "A Dialogue of Self and Soul," Yeats wrote,

> When such as I cast out remorse
> So great a sweetness flows into the breast
> We must laugh and we must sing,
> We are blest by everything,
> Everything we look upon is blest.

While the result of reconcilement may seem madness, the poem is an alchemical fire: the poet goes into it, perhaps serious, aware of the dangers; yet, the poet comes out blessed by the occasion, laughing and singing.

Ellmann puts it this way:

> A man is welded to his image, a player to his role; when we speak of the drama of a heroic action our language is no more figurative than when we speak of its reality. Yeats does not escape his own symbols, but is caught up into them also, and in the poem "High Talk" he describes himself as Malachi Stilt-Jack, and insists that the stilts are part of him as much as his body is, and that, on the other hand, both are also metaphor: "All metaphor, Malachi, stilts and all." All that he has thought and created is part of him, substantiated as his flesh. (*Yeats* 281)

However, Malachi is also a metaphor for all high-talking poets who learn and let what they have learned "run wild" through their poetry. The act of poetry is an act of message, constructed on the ground with chisel and plane, and elevated to make us scream with delight at the ecstacy it gives us and the courage it provides us should we decide to leave our darkness.

Malachi as scholar might suggest that the proper vehicle by which poets may pierce the "stretches of night," bringing them to where "night splits and the dawn breaks loose," is metaphor. This Malachi would say that other scholars ought to "stalk on, stalk on," "through the terrible novelty of light," to find what metaphor might reveal. Certainly, metaphor is not the only way to read a text. However, metaphor is certainly a most reliable, consistently revealing way by which we might solve a poem's riddle. Part of Yeats's greatness, Snukal says, is "his ability to think through his position, and to see connections that most of us have not been prepared to see, and so to deliver us into a world that is a complex whole" (237). Part of metaphor's greatness is that it makes connections that conventional criticism might not prepare us to find; it helps the poet to think through one's interpretive positions while it enables the reader to understand the apparatus of the poet's thought and technique. Thus, when we find ourselves at a poem's end, we see through metaphor the unity of the individual poem as well as its unified place among virtually all the poet's work. Because of metaphor, we might arise from a critical labyrinth, experience the rejoice of the voice "Out of Cavern" ("The Gyres") when at last we understand, when at last we are "riddled with light."

NOTES

Chapter 1:

[1] The poems of this study are cited from: Finneran, Richard J. *W. B. Yeats: The Poems*. New York: Macmillan, 1983.

[2]Anyone who reads Stevens's poetry can see estrangement working, especially in poems such as "Le Monocle de Mon Oncle":

> Like a dull scholar, I behold, in love,
> An ancient aspect touching a new mind.
> It comes, it blooms, it bears the fruit and dies.
> This trivial trope reveals a way of truth.
> Our bloom is gone. We are the fruit thereof.
> Two golden gourds distended on our vines,
> Into the autumn weather, splashed with frost,
> Distorted by hale fatness, turned grotesque.
> We hang like warty squashes, streaked and rayed,
> The laughing sky will see the two of us
> Washed into rinds by rotting winter rains.

While aging and weather in comparison is an old metaphor, Stevens defamiliarizes this when he combines the old with the unfamiliar: the aging couple as "grotesque" vegetation.

[3] Another exceptional example of the type of thing I am discussing here may be in Sylvia Plath's "Mirror." Plath's task was no simple one. The moment she personifies the mirror in the first stanza, she must shape everything in the poem to be consistent to that mirror's personality. The first stanza is an example of the similarity Jakobson spoke of. The mirror reflects, quite literally and figuratively: "Whatever I see I swallow immediately/Just as it is, unmisted by love or dislike." It considers its physical properties: it is "silver and exact," it swallows what it sees without emotion, and, metaphorically, it is the "eye of a little god." This similarity is contrasted by the second stanza's dissimilarity. A mirror, realistically, is flat; however, in the second stanza the mirror is a lake: it has depth, "reaches," and a woman who brings emotion ("tears and an agitation of hands") to it. Consider, too, the metaphorical sequences: the mirror is a mirror; the mirror is a god; the mirror becomes a lake; the god is a lake (and, likely, the "agitation of hands" might be hands joined in prayer). Similarly, the woman is a young girl; the young girl drowned is an old woman; the old woman is a terrible fish. The contrasting of similarity to dissimilarity is the genius of this poem.

[4] For another example of this concept in operation, consider Theodore Roethke's "My Papa's Waltz." The second stanza of the poem illustrates the "sound texture" metaphor especially well:

> We romped until the pans
> Slid from the kitchen shelf;
> My mother's countenance
> Could not unfrown itself.

The sound in certain of these words is metaphorical. *Romp*, for example, is playful, short, and upbeat. *Countenance*, on the other hand, sounds heavy; it is polysyllabic, and this makes it feel serious. As well, the rhythm in the word descends rather than lifts. Papa's waltz, a low-level, drunken dance, matches the low-level diction of the word *romped*; "mother's countenance" matches in its high-level diction her place as the authority in the family. The metaphors found here could not have happened if Roethke had chosen to write, "My mother's face / Could not stop frowning."

[5] For more information on Yeats's use of the pun and Maud Gonne, refer to: Billiet, Conrad. "W. B. Yeats: The Pun of a Gonne." *Modern British Literature* 4 (1979): 44-50.

[6] Looking again at Roethke's "My Papa's Waltz," one will find the poet substituting several times. Each time creates metrical metaphor. Examine a scansion of the following lines:

> ˘ ´ ˘ ´ ˘ ´
> We romped | until | the pans
> ´ ˘ ˘ ´ ˘ ´
> Slid from | the kit | chen shelf.

Although the poem is written in iambic trimeter, the trochee ("Slid from") draws our attention to the metrical shift. Metaphorically, as the pans slide from the shelf, the trochee slides from accent to unaccent (Wallace 68).

[7] To see what Roman Jakobson does with this concept, see "Yeats's 'Sorrow of Love' Through the Years," Selected Writings, 3: 607-09.

[8] For another example of "grammatical equivalences" as metaphorical strategy, Roethke's "Dolor" provides us with numerous examples:

> I have known the inexorable sadness of pencils,
> Neat in their boxes, dolor of pad and paper-weight,
> All the misery of manilla folders and mucilage,
> Desolation in immaculate public places,

Lonely reception room, lavatory, switchboard,
The unalterable pathos of basin and pitcher,
Ritual of multigraph, paper-clip, comma,
Endless duplication of lives and objects.
And I have seen dust from the walls of institutions,
Finer than flour, alive, more dangerous than silica,
Sift, almost invisible, through long afternoons of tedium,
Dropping a fine film on nails and delicate eyebrows,
Glazing the pale hair, the duplicate grey standard faces.

Doing what Jakobson suggests, we can chart the following combinations:

Abstract Nouns	Prepositions	Concrete/Personal Noun
inexorable sadness	of	pencils
dolor	of	pad and paper-weight
misery	of	manilla folders and mucilage
desolation	in	immaculate public places, lonely reception room, lavatory, switchboard
unalterable pathos	of	basin and pitcher
ritual	of	multigraph, paper-clip, comma
endless duplication	of	lives and objects

In lines 9-11, Roethke shifts the structure by reversing the syntactical order. There, the combinations are:

Concrete/Personal Nouns	Prepositions	Abstract Nouns
dust	from	walls of institutions
long afternoons	of	tedium

Then, he shifts back to the original pattern in the last line:

Abstract Noun	Preposition	Concrete/Personal Nouns
fine film	on	nails, delicate eyebrows,
pale		hair, grey standard faces

We have in this poem a wealthy distribution of abstract nouns to concrete nouns. An interesting thing occurs, here, too: the first three combinations are joined by the preposition *of*; during the fourth combination, Roethke changes the preposition to *in* while retaining the same grammatical structure. What is the significance of the change in preposition? Besides establishing variance for the reader's sake, it diverts our attention from the objects to locations occupied by people. The reader will also note the number of objects increases in the concrete/personal column. This builds as we read, overloading the imagery until Roethke has created a pathetic drama of the lives of people as represented metaphorically by pencils and envelopes.

When Roethke renews his use of the *of* preposition, you will find the number here equal to the of prepositions preceding the use of *in*. Metaphorically, these signify the duplication of the pattern as well as the duplication of "lives and objects." Even when Roethke changes the structure by reversing the order, it is continued duplication for the grammatical units have not changed. The final reversal, and the heaviest grouping of concrete/personal nouns, intensifies the metaphor a final time.

[9] For further grammatical analysis of Yeats's poetry, refer to: Adams, Joseph. *Yeats and the Masks of Syntax*. New York: Columbia UP, 1984.

[10] I derive this sentence from the first book of Genesis and from John 1: 1-5. According to Scriptures, God commanded the creation of the world; God spoke it into existence. The poet's task, as I see it, involves a good amount of self-creation.

Chapter 2:

[1] Among the writers of the 18th century who seem to have had some influence upon Yeats's work, either directly or indirectly, are James Thomson, Oliver Goldsmith, William Cowper, Thomas Gray, and Robert Burns. Thomson's "The Seasons," Gray's "Elegy Written in a Country Church-yard," Goldsmith's "The Deserted Village," and Cowper's "The Task" seem to influence the pastoral element of Yeats's early poetry; sometimes, certain images seem borrowed from these particular poems. Burns's Scottish nationalism, of course, reminds one of Yeats's Irish nationalism. Other writers I have in mind include Spenser, whose influence Yeats notes.

[2] My interpretation of "The Song of the Happy Shepherd" and "The Sad Shepherd" arose from seminar discussions with Dr. Linda Pratt of the University of Nebraska-Lincoln.

[3] I refer here to points quoted in Chapter 1 from Derrida's *Of Grammatology* (37, 67).

[4] Many of the poems from Blake's *Songs of Innocence* and *Songs of Experience* would serve as examples, including the companion poems "The Little Boy Lost" and "The Little Boy Found" juxtaposed to "The Little Girl Lost" and "The Little Girl Found." Obviously, Blake's antithetical structures heavily influenced

Yeats's work.

[5] In case the reader does not know the story, Yeats describes the inception of "The Lake Isle of Innisfree" in his *Autobiography*:

> I had still the ambition, formed in Sligo in my teens, of living in imitation of Thoreau on Innisfree, a little island in Lough Gill, and when walking through Fleet Street very homesick I heard a little tinkle of water and saw a fountain in a shop-window which balanced a little ball upon its jet, and began to remember lake water. From the sudden remembrance came my poem Innisfree, my first lyric with anything in its rhythm of my own music. (103)

[6] Yeats devises his own web some years after these poems in *A Vision*. The concentric cones and Great Wheel as illustrated in that book look very much like some sort of web. See *A Vision* (81, 199-201, 266).

[7] Blake writes in "The Marriage of Heaven and Hell":

> Without Contraries is no progression. Attraction and Repulsion, Reason and Energy, Love and Hate, are necessary to Human existence.
>
> From these contraries spring what the religious call Good & Evil. Good is the passive that obeys Reason[.] Evil is the active springing from Energy.
>
> Good is Heaven. Evil is Hell.

Yeats recognizes, I think, the duality of our existences. The reconciliation he seeks for is not, really, a favoring of one extreme over the other. Rather, reconcilement is the merging of these oppositions; from that, and the acceptance of extremities as they influence our lives, a sort of antithetical peace ensues.

[8] This line is of essential note, since it brings to mind "The Second Coming's" "blood-dimmed tides." Here, Yeats shows how beauty's presence is lost in the futility of mankind's warring; it exists, but humankind fails to see it. In "The Second Coming," beauty of a specific kind will be born out of violence.

[9] Refer to my earlier web analogy in this chapter. Much the same thing occurs here.

[10] I have modified this phrase from Matthew 16: 25: "For whoever wants to save his life will lose it, but whoever loses his life for me will find it" (NIV). The phrase, as I use it, bears a cyclical notion beyond the Christian paradox. Life brings with it death; death begins with life. In the case of the Rose, to pursue it is to lose it; to lose the Rose, is to find it.

[11] I am thinking here of Byron's "Manfred," the end of Act II. The meeting Manfred has with Astarte is very close to the scene Yeats portrays in "The Song

of Wandering Aengus." Other of Yeats's poems remind me of "Manfred," too. "Manfred's" Magian brings to mind Yeats's "The Magi"; "Manfred's" tower brings to mind all of Yeats's; Manfred's confrontation with the Abbot brings to mind Crazy Jane's meetings with the Bishop.

[12] I call the old men "rough beasts" because of their composite descriptions. The "rough beast" in "The Second Coming" was, also, a composite creature.

[13] Take note of the final lines of "The Two Trees":

> There, through the broken branches, go
> The ravens of unresting thought;
> Flying, crying, to and fro,
> Cruel claw and hungry throat,
> Or else they stand and sniff the wind,
> And shake their ragged wings; . . .

What I find significant about these lines is how the image of the ravens, coupled with the previous mention of "gyring," brings to mind Yeats's "The Second Coming." The ravens are carrion birds, much like the "indignant desert birds" that reel above the "rough beast." As well, consider the nature of the bird in its metaphorical relationship to philosophy, the dying thoughts. The carrion bird feeds upon the rotting flesh of passing thought.

Chapter 3:

[1] See "The Three Beggars," "The Three Hermits," "Beggar to Beggar Cried," and "Running to Paradise."

[2] "Passionate intensity" is taken, obviously, from "The Second Coming." The term *anima bruta* is borrowed from Allen R. Grossman's *Poetic Knowledge in the Early Yeats: A Study of* The Wind Among the Reeds. Grossman writes:

> When in "Leda and the Swan" the god descends upon the girl, Yeats says she is mastered "by the brute blood of the air," which communicates through her to the world not knowledge but violence.The phrase is a somewhat extended translation of the *anima bruta* which Yeats found in the discussion of the powers of air in Kingsford and Maitland's *The Perfect Way*, an early book of the theosophical movement and one which was almost omnipotent in the eighties when Yeats received the most lasting elements of his education. The *anima bruta* is an aspect of the astral body (or *anima mundi*). (54)

[3] When I was in grade school and high school, I was a pigeon hobbiest and

raised exotic breeds of pigeons in a loft in my backyard. The loft would literally thunder during the mating and courtship rituals. I am also taken by the sexual metaphor implicit in the bee imagery. Flowers pollinate with the bees' assistance. The dipping in and out of the flowers with their oblong bodies is, in many respects, equivalent to copulation.

[4] Of course, the "blood" emblem attributed to bats is severely inaccurate. Few bat species seek blood for sustenance. Most are fruit and insect eaters.

[5] As noted in Chapter 2, Beauty is eternal. Here, Passion is eternal. We might do well to consider the mathematical equation inherent in metaphor. Is Beauty equal to Passion? Is Passion, perhaps, yet another road to the Rose?

[6] See 1 Kings 4: 29-34 of the Old Testament for an account of Solomon's wisdom.

[7] I am thinking here of the fires of Pentecost, though obviously Solomon's time would have predated that event. What I am referring to is the unknown prayer or spiritual language of New Testament tongues. Acts 2: 1-4 and Acts 2: 14-21 of the New Testament describe how the Holy Spirit descended upon the apostles and how they began speaking in tongues. This event marked the original surge of Christian evangelism. If Sheba has been given a prayer language, it comes from the religious or spiritual significance of the sexual act. This is obviously not orthodox Judeo-Christianity, but sexual union is equivalent to mandalic unity. I have been discussing how Yeats uses metaphor to bridge the physical world to the imaginative, thus completing the universe. Why cannot the sex act also construct a bridge to make the circle of existence complete?

[8] See section 124 of Tennyson's poem. Tennyson did much the thing Yeats is endeavoring to do. Tennyson is left in the mortal world while his friend Hallam, who is dead, is in the non-mortal world. Tennyson's poem repudiates any concept of Heaven but not necessarily the existence of a visionary world. Despite the fact he "heard a voice, 'believe no more,'" and that he refers to the "Godless deep," Tennyson understands the duality of physical and spiritual existence. He has felt and heard the temporary presence of his dead friend, returned to him. He has felt the sensation of the spiritual and visionary experience, and this feeling is enough.

[9] See Judges 15: 15-17 for Samson's defense against the Philistines.

[10] I wonder if Yeats intends a bit of subtle humor by referring to the collar-bone of a hare. Considering the sexual overtones often found in the anima bruta metaphor, the hare is certainly an appropriate, procreative and potent creature.

[11] See Hebrews 13: 8—"Jesus Christ is the same yesterday and today and forever" (NIV).

[12] I do not mean "prophetic" in the popular definition—that prophecy foretells or predicts the future. I refer to it as a spiritual gift of wisdom, an

utterance of a persistent truth meant to edify a body of believers, in much the same fashion certain modern charismatic Christians use the term. Obviously, Yeats's prophecy is not Christian, though spiritually his sense of the prophetic is equivalent. For further orthodox information refer to 1 Corinthians 13: 2.

[13] See Yeats's *Autobiography* (128, 166) for discussions about the Unity of Being.

[14] For more direct information on the concept of concentric cones, refer to Yeats's *A Vision*, particularly the text of "Part I: The Principal Symbol" of "Book I: The Great Wheel," and "Book II: The Completed Symbol." Refer also to the illustration of "The Historical Cones" (266).

[15] Recall the discussion of "white foam" at the beginning of this chapter. "White rush" suggests not just the rush of emotions but the rush of the ejaculate toward the ovum.

[16] This brings to mind what Yeats wrote in "A Dialogue of Self and Soul": "I am content to live it all again."

[17] I wonder if Yeats has in mind "The Cat and the Moon," which deals directly with the moon's phases. If "The Cat and the Moon" deals metaphorically with God's unchanging and needful changing characteristics, can we suppose the old moon refers to the outgoing model of god, which is unwavering and rational, and the arrival of the new god which is more animal, as the "horn" reference connotes?

[18] A good bit of irony occurs in this poem. Michael Robartes and the dancer seem anything but "blest" because the characters have let themselves step outside the vision of the earlier poem, "The Double Vision of Michael Robartes." They interpret and analyze too much, especially Robartes, who examines things too clinically, to escape the corrupting intellect. The dancer generally responds in a disinterested fashion, which separates her from her more consumed sexual counterpart. Robartes talks about a lady whose "half-dead dragon was her thought," and the dancer later says, "My wretched dragon is perplexed." One, her thoughts are perplexed; two, Robartes, who seems to be putting his thoughts into her head, is perplexed. Robartes speaks truth when he says that "blest souls are not composite." Ironically, the speaker at this point is most pathetically composite. Then again, the dancer is not dancing in this poem either. Perhaps the dance ought to "outdance thought" as it had in "The Double Vision of Michael Robartes."

[19] The first two quotes come from "Easter 1916"; the last comes from "The Cat and the Moon."

[20] The sex of the Sphinx creature is changed in "The Second Coming" from female to male. In "The Double Vision of Michael Robartes," the Sphinx had "woman breast and lion paw." Furthermore, just as the "rough beast" has "a gaze blank and pitiless as the sun," the Sphinx in "The Double Vision

of Michael Robartes" "gazed upon all things known, all things unknown, / In triumph of intellect / With motionless head erect."

Chapter 4:

[1] Recall, too, the list of Yeats's countrymen and friends mentioned in such later poems as "In Memory of Major Robert Gregory" and "Easter 1916."

[2] We might excuse the myopicism of Bohlmann's "historical"; however, he also says,

> the "pale unsatisfied ones" hope "to find once more" "The uncontrollable mystery on the bestial floor," the kind of irrationality which characterized a previous age. Christianity, constricting man in "stiff, painted clothes," is not a one-time phenomenon destined to endure in a single form for ever; its impulse will be superseded by one of opposite tincture, just as "Calvary's turbulence" wrecked the age that went before it. The end of any cycle is accompanied by turbulence and "loss of control," as "the whole thing turns bottom upwards" . . . . (177)

Bohlmann's interpretation may not be entirely incorrect; however, he tends to simplify a very complex poem with the easiest and most accessible reading.

[3] The image of "the blue depth of sky" is similar to Wallace Stevens's use of blue. Blue is Stevens's color for transforming awareness, as in "Man with a Blue Guitar."

[4] Hamlet's hesitance to act comes often, as in Act III, scene iii (lines 73-95) or in Act IV, scene iv (lines 33-66).

[5] See Chapter 3 where I analyze "The Cat and the Moon" at length.

Chapter 5

[1] Bloom writes, "Famous as the last stanza is, one wonders at calling a generation 'the last romantics' whose chosen theme was 'traditional sanctity and loveliness.' Is that 'whatever most can bless / The mind of man or elevate a rhyme'?" (382). Bloom's sense of the appositive used to modify theme is pathetically miscued. "[W]hatever most can bless" is as much an apposite for *theme* as "Traditional sanctity and loveliness." It is definitely not modification of the second line, as he seems to suppose.

[2] This is like King Guaire's question asked of the three beggars in "The Three Beggars."

[3] Notice the similarities of this concept to the opening stanza of "Sailing to Byzantium."

[4] See "The Cold Heaven."

[5] I take the phrase "abundant life" from a Biblical source: John 10: 10 (KJ). Yeats, of course, does not allude to Biblical values here, though the phrase seems to fit even Yeats's secularized example.

[6] See Luke 21: 27 and, particularly, 1 Thessalonians 4: 15-17.

[7] Certain of the elements bear resemblance to Shelley's "Mont Blanc," Milton's *Paradise Lost*, Tennyson's "The Palace of Art," and Coleridge's "Kubla Khan."

Chapter 6:

[1]Bernard Levine uses this discussion as the basis for the title of his *The Dissolving Image: The Spiritual-Esthetic Development of W. B. Yeats*. Levine's notion of the "dissolving image" is about external poetic forms being dissolved into the soul of poetry (9-10), and how outside ideas dissolve and transform into art. Levine's study does not deal with the metaphor of dissolution.

[2] I have trouble with this particular word, *immature*. Yeats's poetry never strikes me as being really immature. His earliest poetry exhibits a great deal of maturity, manifested in serious use of craft and complex thought. Even so, it often cannot compare to the product of his later years. Yeats had not yet examined the "desolation of reality" in the earlier poetry, thus it simply does not enter into his discourse. Does this mean immaturity? Probably not, though if we measure maturity as the result of the accumulation of experience, then the early work is immature.

[3] "The Lamentation of the Old Pensioner" appears in *The Collected Poems of William Butler Yeats* as part of *The Rose* collection, published in 1893. However, this poem is a 1925 rewrite of "The Old Pensioner," originally published in *The Rose*. For comparative purposes, the text of "The Old Pensioner" follows:

> I had a chair at every hearth,
> When no one turned to see
> With "Look at the old fellow there;
> And who may he be?"
> And therefore do I wander on,
> And the fret is on me.
>
> The road-side trees keep murmuring—
> Ah, wherefore murmur ye

As in the old days long gone by,
Green oak and poplar tree!
The well-known faces are all gone,
And the fret is on me.

(Garab 10)

Chapter 7:

[1] In *A Vision*, Blake's position on "The Great Wheel" is Phase Sixteen (137-40); Yeats's position belongs to Phase Seventeen (140-45). Phase Sixteen is higher than Phase Seventeen.

[2] See Chapter Five for my discussions on "Sailing to Byzantium" and "Byzantium."

[3] "Daddy-long-legs," metaphorically the poet upon stilts, conjures the image of a spider, exciting enough for children. One wonders if "Daddy-long-legs" suggests something about the poetic web a poet weaves. Refer to Chapter Two where I discuss the poetic web and its relationship to "The Rose."

[4] This brings to mind Tennyson's "The Lady of Shalott." The Lady "weaveth constantly" and can only view the world through a mirrored image. When she views the world directly, the mirror cracks and she believes she is cursed and dies. Here, obviously, the women in the upper stories, in their towers (so to speak), are looking for a reason to look out the window to relieve them of their mundane labors of patching. The image is similar, but the mirror and the gaze outward have different results. One succumbs to her own fears, whereas the "High Talk" ladies find joy even in their fright. The stilted procession makes life worth the living.

[5] This is a curious change, though thematically it holds consistently to the poet's deliberate craftsmanship. Where once Yeats viewed poetry as equivalent to the act of making clothing ("Adam's Curse" and "A Coat"), he now views it as more physical labor—not a needle, but hammers, chisels, and planes. Then again, Yeats's subjects seem less delicate fabric than they once did.

[6] The following is Finneran's note on Malachi:

> Malachi ("my messenger") is the supposed author of the last book of the Old Testament in the Bible; St. Malachy (1095-1148) is an Irish saint, known for his reforms; Malachi Mulligan is the name applied to Yeats's friend Oliver St. John Gogarty (1878-1957) by James Joyce (1882-1941) in *Ulysses.*

[7] I have taken some liberties with Mulryne's quote and only used that

portion which made sense. The entire quotation is as follows (italics are mine):

> Yeats casts himself as Malachi-Stilt Jack, the maker of metaphors, of art in the grand manner. *Already implicit in the chosen dramatis persona is an ironic valuation: the walker upon stilts, though an eye-catching figure, is inescapably an absurd posturing creature on his "timber toes"; the reaction he provokes from the onlookers recalls only juvenile practical jokes: "women shriek."* And the activity he is committed to is a precarious one, carried out unnaturally, under strain. *The last few lines of the poem record with desperate seriousness the human predicament from which attention has been diverted by the stilted figure. Metaphor, the poet's craft, is explicitly abandoned. The setting registers apocalypse: "night splits and the dawn breaks loose"; but it brings with it "terrible novelty," not the welcome of a conquered territory.*

Mulryne may be correct in some instances, but he veers off that course and lands into some very wrong-headed explication. The walking on stilts is far from "juvenile practical jokes." It is a precarious business, with the very serious purpose of making the women shriek for reasons I have suggested in this chapter. Mulryne mistakenly makes the women's responses childish. After all, the women demanded the "face at the pane." Mulryne also makes the ending of the poem too serious, turning what is meant to be joy in the face of apocalypse into something dreadful. There is no dread; granted, the experience may be a "terrible novelty," but Mulryne omits the very important, illuminating completion of the phrase: "terrible novelty of light." The poet will "stalk on, stalk on," continue the metaphorical search that never ends. As any poet knows, there is no "welcome of conquered territory." Yeats shows time and time again how the poet is a hero, going out to conquer territories, not to settle on territories already conquered by someone else, or even himself. As I noted in Chapter 1, Yeats said that "no man can do the same thing twice if he has put much mind into it" (*Explorations* 430).

WORKS CITED

Albright, Daniel. *The Myth Against Myth: A Study of Yeats's Imagination in Old Age.* London: Oxford UP, 1972.

Bachchan, Harbans Rai. *W. B. Yeats and Occultism: A Study of His Works in Relation to Indian Lore, the Cabbala, Swedenborg, Boehme and Theosophy.* 1965. London: Books from India, 1976.

Barthes, Roland. "The Structuralist Activity." Davis 302-06.

Bloom, Harold. *Yeats.* New York: Oxford UP, 1970.

Bohlmann, Otto. *Yeats and Nietzsche: An Exploration of Major Nietzschean Echoes in the Writings of William Butler Yeats.* Totowa: Barnes & Noble, 1982.

Booth, Wayne C. "Metaphor as Rhetoric: The Problem of Evaluation." Sacks 47-70.

Bradford, Curtis B. *Yeats at Work.* Carbondale: Southern Illinois UP, 1965.

Burke, Kenneth. *Perspectives by Incongruity.* Ed. Stanley Edgar Hyman. Bloomington: Indiana UP, 1964.

Byrd, Thomas L., Jr. *The Early Poetry of W. B. Yeats: The Poetic Quest.* Port Washington, London: Kennikat, 1978.

Chatterjee, Bhabatosh. *The Poetry of W. B. Yeats.* Calcutta: Orient Longmans, 1962.

Clougherty, Robert James, Jr. *The History of Three Irish Poets: W.B. Yeats, Seamus Heaney, and Richard Murphy.* Diss. Tulsa U, 1991.

Daiches, David. "The Earlier Poems: Some Themes and Patterns." Jeffares and Cross 48-67.

Davidson, Donald. "What Metaphors Mean." Sacks 29-45.

Davie, Donald. "'Michael Robartes and the Dancer.'" Donoghue and Mulryne 73-87.

Davis, Robert Con, ed. *Contemporary Literary Criticism: Modernism Through Poststructuralism.* New York: Longman, 1986.

Derrida, Jacques. *Of Grammatology.* Trans. Gayatri Chakravorty Spivak. 1967. Baltimore: Johns Hopkins UP, 1976.

---. "Structure, Sign, and Play in the Discourse of Human Sciences." Davis 480-98.

Donoghue, Denis, and J. R. Mulryne. *An Honored Guest.* New York: St. Martin's, 1966.

Ellmann, Richard. *Eminent Domain: Yeats Among Wilde, Joyce, Pound, Eliot, and Auden.* New York: Oxford UP, 1967.

---. *The Identity of Yeats.* New York: Oxford UP, 1964.

---. *Yeats: The Man and the Masks.* New York: E. P. Dutton, 1948.

Ellmann, Richard, and Robert O'Clair, eds. *The Norton Anthology of Modern Poetry.* New York: Norton, 1973.

Engelberg, Edward. "'He Too was in Arcadia': Yeats and the Paradox of the Fortunate Fall." Jeffares and Cross 69-92.
---. *The Vast Design: Patterns in W. B. Yeats's Aesthetic.* Toronto: U of Toronto P, 1964.
Erlich, Victor. *Russian Formalism: History & Doctrine.* The Hague: Mouton, 1969.
Finneran, Richard J, ed. *W. B. Yeats: The Poems.* New York: Macmillan, 1983.
---. Vol. 5 of *Yeats: An Annual of Critical and Textual Studies.* Ann Arbor; London: U.M.I. Research, 1987.
Friedman, Barton R. *Adventures in the Deeps of the Mind: The Cuchulain Cycle of W. B. Yeats.* Princeton: Princeton UP, 1977.
Frye, Northrup. "The Rising of the Moon: A Study of 'A Vision.'" Donoghue and Mulryne 8-33.
Garab, Arra M. *Beyond Byzantium: The Last Phase of Yeats's Career.* DeKalb: Northern Illinois UP, 1969.
Garratt, Robert F. *Modern Irish Poetry: Tradition and Continuity from Yeats to Heaney.* Berkeley: U of California P, 1986.
Grossman, Allen R. *Poetic Knowledge in the Early Yeats: A Study of* The Wind Among the Reeds. Charlottesville: UP of Virginia, 1969.
Harris, Daniel A. *Yeats: Coole Park & Ballylee.* Baltimore; London: Johns Hopkins UP, 1974.
Hassett, Joseph M. *Yeats and the Poetics of Hate.* Dublin: Gill and Martin; New York: St. Martin's, 1986.
Henn, T. R. "'The Green Helmet' and 'Responsibilities.'" Donoghue and Mulryne 34-53.
---. *The Lonely Tower: Studies in the Poetry of W. B. Yeats.* 1950. London: Methuen, 1966.
Hopkins, Gerard Manley. *The Journals and Papers.* London: Oxford UP, 1959.
Jakobson, Roman. *The Framework of Language.* N.p.: Michigan Studies, 1980.
---. *Selected Writings.* Ed. Stephen Rudy. 7 vols. New York: Mouton, 1971-81.
Jeffares, A. Norman. *The Circus Animals: Essays on W. B. Yeats.* Stanford: Stanford UP, 1970.
---. *A Commentary on the Collected Poems of W. B. Yeats.* Stanford: Stanford UP, 1968.
Jeffares, A. Norman, and K. G. W. Cross. *In Excited Reverie: A Centenary Tribute to William Butler Yeats 1865-1939.* New York: Macmillan, 1965.
Jordan, Carmel. *A Terrible Beauty: The Easter Rebellion and Yeats's "Great Tapestry."* Lewisburg: Bucknell UP; London and Toronto: Associated UP, 1987.
Kermode, Frank. *Romantic Image.* New York: Vintage, 1957.
Koch, Vivienne. *W. B. Yeats: The Tragic Phase.* 1951. N.p.: Archon, 1969.
Komesu, Okifumi. *The Double Perspective of Yeats's Aesthetic.* Gerrards Cross, Bucks: Colin Smythe; Totowa: Barnes & Noble, 1984.

Lense, Edward. "Sailing the Seas to Nowhere: Inversions of Yeats's Symbolism in 'Sailing to Byzantium.'" Finneran 95-106.
Levine, Bernard. *The Dissolving Image: The Spiritual-Esthetic Development of W. B. Yeats.* Detroit: Wayne State UP, 1970.
Martin, Graham. "'The Wild Swans at Coole.'" Donoghue and Mulryne 54-72.
Melchiori, Giorgio. *The Whole Mystery of Art: Pattern into Poetry in the Work of W. B. Yeats.* London: Routledge & Kegan Paul, 1960.
Mulryne, J. R. "The 'Last Poems.'" Donoghe and Mulryne 124-42.
Nietzsche, Friedrich. "On Truth and Falsity in Their Extramoral Sense." Shibles 1-13.
Oppel, Frances Nesbitt. *Masks and Tragedy: Yeats and Nietzsche, 1902-10.* Charlottesville: UP of Virginia, 1987.
Parkin, Andrew. *The Dramatic Imagination of W. B. Yeats.* Dublin: Gill & Macmillan; New York: Barnes & Noble, 1978.
Peterson, Richard F. *William Butler Yeats.* Boston: Twayne, 1982.
Poulet, Georges. "Phenomenology of Reading." Davis 350-62.
Rajan, Balachandra. *W. B. Yeats: A Critical Introduction.* London: Hutchinson U Library, 1965.
Reid, B. L. William Butler Yeats: *The Lyric of Tragedy.* Norman: U of Oklahoma P, 1961.
Ricoeur, Paul. "The Metaphorical Process on Cognition, Imagination, and Feeling." Sacks 141-57.
Rosenthal, M. L., ed. *Selected Poems and Two Plays of William Butler Yeats.* 1962. New York: Collier, 1973.
Sacks, Sheldon, ed. *On Metaphor.* Chicago: U of Chicago P, 1979.
Shibles, Warren, ed. *Essays on Metaphor.* Whitewater: Language, 1972.
Shklovsky, Viktor. "Art as Technique." Davis 52-63.
Smith, Peter Alderson. *W. B. Yeats and the Tribes of Danu: Three Views of Ireland's Fairies.* Gerrards Cross, Bucks: Colin Smythe; Totowa: Barnes & Noble, 1987.
Snukal, Robert. *High Talk: The Philosophical Poetry of W. B. Yeats.* London: Cambridge UP, 1973.
Stacy, R. H. *Defamiliarization in Language and Literature.* Syracuse: Syracuse UP, 1977.
Stevens, Wallace. *The Necessary Angel: Essays on Reality and the Imagination.* 1942. New York: Vintage, 1951.
Stock, A. G. *W. B. Yeats: His Poetry and Thought.* Cambridge: Cambridge UP, 1961.
Symons, Arthur. *The Symbolist Movement in Literature.* 1919. New York: Dutton, 1958.
Unterecker, John. *A Reader's Guide to William Butler Yeats.* New York: Farrar,

Straus, & Giroux, 1959.
Wade, Allan, ed. *The Letters of W. B. Yeats.* London: Rupert Hart-Davis, 1954.
Wallace, Robert. *Writing Poems.* 2nd ed. Boston: Little, Brown, 1987.
Whitaker, Thomas R. *Swan and Shadow: Yeats's Dialogue with History.* Chapel Hill: U of North Carolina P, 1964.
Wilson, Edmund. *Axel's Castle: A Study in the Imaginative Literature of 1870-1930.* New York: Scribner's, 1931.
Wimsatt, W. K., Jr., and Monroe Beardsley. "The Intentional Fallacy." Davis 78-88.
Yeats, W. B. *The Autobiography of William Butler Yeats.* 1916. New York: Collier, 1965.
---. *Essays and Introductions.* New York: Macmillan, 1961.
---. *Explorations.* New York: Macmillan, 1962.
---. *Mythologies.* New York: Macmillan, 1959.
---. *The Oxford Book of Modern Verse: 1892-1935.* New York: Oxford UP, 1936.
---. *Uncollected Prose.* Eds. John P. Frayne and Colton Johnson. 2 vols. New York: Columbia UP, 1976.
---. *The Variorum Edition of the Poems.* Eds. P. Allt and R. K. Alspach. New York: Macmillan, 1957.
---. *A Vision.* New York: Collier, 1937.
Young, David. *Troubled Mirror: A Study of Yeats's The Tower.* Iowa City: U of Iowa P, 1987.
Zwerdling, Alex. "W. B. Yeats: Variations on the Visionary Quest." Unterecker 80-92.
---. *Yeats and the Heroic Ideal.* New York: New York UP, 1965.

INDEX

Albright, Daniel, 58, 143
Aristotle, 129
Arnold, Matthew, 123

Bachchan, Harbans Rai, 40, 46, 51
Barthes, Roland, 30
Bastien-Lepage, Jules, 85
Bible, The
    Genesis, 153
    Judges, 156
    1 Kings, 156
    Acts 2 (Pentecost), 156
    1 Corinthians, 157
    Hebrews, 156
    John, 153, 159
    Luke, 159
    Matthew, 154
    1 Thessalonians, 157
Blake, William, 9, 11, 37, 48, 87, 143, 153, 154, 160
    "Little Boy Found, The," 153
    "Little Boy Lost, The," 153
    "Little Girl Found, The," 153
    "Little Girl Lost, The," 153
    "Marriage of Heaven and Hell, The," 154
    Songs of Experience, 153
    Songs of Innocence, 153
Bloom, Harold, 71, 82, 94, 95, 96, 102, 103, 105, 121, 128, 131, 132, 134, 135, 136, 137, 158
Bohlman, Otto, 91, 92, 158
Booth, Wayne C., 21, 29
Bradford, Curtis B., 138
Browning, Robert, 117
Burke, Edmund, 114
Burke, Kenneth, 20
Burns, Robert, 153
Byrd, Thomas L., Jr., 39, 41, 43, 50-51
Byron, George Gordon Lord, 53, 154
    "Manfred," 154, 155

Chain of Being, 24
Chatterjee, Bhabatosh, 113
Christianity (or *Judeo-Christian*, or *Christ*), 81, 82, 91, 92, 97, 98, 114, 116, 129, 134, 154, 156, 157, 158, 159
Clougherty, Robert James Jr., 122
Coleridge, Samuel Taylor, 36, 104, 114, 115, 116, 117, 159
"This Lime Tree Bower My Prison," 36
"Kubla Khan," 104, 114, 115, 116, 117, 159
Cowper, William, 153

Daiches, David, 32-33
Dante (Dante Alighieri), 85
Davidson, Donald, 21
Davie, Donald, 83
Deconstruction, 35
Defamiliarization, 17, 25
Derrida, Jacques, 10, 13, 14, 15, 19, 21, 35, 87, 146, 153
Duran, Carolus, 85

Ellmann, Richard, 61, 62, 68, 69, 72, 73, 74, 87, 94, 101, 115, 121, 125, 129, 130
Ellmann, Richard, and Robert O'Clair, 25
Engelberg, Edward, 88, 107
Erlich, Victor, 18

Finneran, Richard J., 146, 160
Friedman, Barton R., 85, 86
Frye, Northrup, 80

Garrab, Arra, 121, 125, 138
Garratt, Robert F., 122
Garty, Oliver St. John, 160
Goldsmith, Oliver, 153
Gonne, Maud, 25, 60, 67, 68, 74, 75, 109, 129, 130, 132, 138, 151
Grattan, Henry, 114
Gray, Thomas, 153
Gregory, Augusta Lady, 60, 101, 102, 104, 105
Gross, Allen, 59

Hamlet, 95, 135, 158
Harris, Daniel A., 112
Hassett, Joseph M., 135

Henn, T. R., 89, 137
Homer, 133
Hopkins, Gerard Manley, 20, 26
Huxley, Aldous, 85
Hyde-Lees, Georgianna, 61

Irish nationalism, 9, 32, 46, 121, 153

Jakobson, Roman, ?
Jeffares, A. Norman, 81, 82, 138
Jordan, Carmel, 79
Joyce, James, 160
Jung, Carl, 117

Kant, Immanuel, 10, 101
Keats, John, 117
Kermode, Frank, 87, 143
King Lear, 135
Kingsford, Anna Bonus, and Edward Maitland, 155
Knight, Wilson, 117
Komesu, Okifumi, 116

Lense, Edward, 107
Levine, Bernard, 70, 125, 126, 159

Martin, Graham, 65
Melchiori, Giorgio, 116
Milton, John, 114, 117, 159
    Paradise Lost, 159
Modernism, 143
Mulligan, Malachi, 160
Mulryne, J. R., 160

Nietzsche, Friedrich, 19, 80, 91, 122

Oppal, Frances, 87

Parkin, Andrew, 84
Peterson, Richard, 37, 93
Plath, Sylvia, 150
Plato, 129

Pope, Alexander, 24, 117
Poulet, Georges, 29
Pratt, Linda Ray, 153
Pre-Raphaelite, 32
Pythagoras of Samos, 129

Rajan, Balachandra, 138
Reid, B. L. 129, 141
Richards, I. A., 19
Ricoeur, Paul, 20, 21, 29
Rilke, Rainer Maria, 123
Roethke, Theodore, 151, 152, 153
    "Dolor," 151-152
    "My Papa's Waltz," 151
Romanticism, 9, 10, 32, 36, 53, 58, 121, 122, 123, 127, 138, 143
Rosenthal, M. L., 138
Russian formalism, 16, 18

Scottish nationalism, 153
Shelley, Percy Bysshe, 9, 71, 114, 117, 159
    "Mont Blanc," 159
Shklovsky, Viktor, 16, 17, 23
Smith, Peter Alderson, 46-47, 49, 51, 55
Snukal, Robert, 148
Spenser, Edmund, 153
St. Anthony, 98
St. Malachy, 160
St. Simon Stylites, 98
Stevens, Wallace, 15, 18, 101, 107, 121, 122, 133, 150, 158
    "Le Monocle de Mon Oncle," 150
    "Man with a Blue Guitar," 158
Stock, A. G., 81
Swift, Jonathan, 114
Symons, Arthur, 15

Tennyson, Alfred Lord, 64, 114, 117, 122, 159, 160
    "In Memorium A.H.H.," 64
    "Lady of Shalott, The," 160
    "Palace of Art, The," 159
Thomson, James, 153
Tyndall, John, 85

Unity of Being, 68, 69, 79, 85, 91, 94, 98, 119, 131, 134
Unterecker, John, 85, 86

Victorian, 122, 143

Wade, Allan, 123
Wallace, Robert, 151
Whitaker, Thomas R., 80
Wilde, Oscar, 101
Wilson, Edmund, 130
Wimsatt, W. K., and Monroe Beardsley, 13
Wordsworth, William, 142

Yeats (*works*):
"Adam's Curse," 15, 16, 59, 85, 86, 87, 88, 99, 145, 160
"Against Unworthy Praise," 138
"Among School Children," 25, 33, 52, 55, 67, 68-69, 71, 72, 74, 75, 79, 87, 129, 131, 146
"Anashuya and Vijaya," 33
"Apparitions, The," 136, 146
"Are You Content?" 120, 121, 132
Autobiography, 85, 98, 154, 157
"Beggar to Beggar Cried," 57, 155
"Black Tower, The," 113-114
"Blood and the Moon," 72, 113
"Byzantium," 15, 16, 21, 30, 120, 125, 137
"Cat and the Moon, The," 65-66-67, 68, 72, 79, 97, 116, 140, 157, 158
"Circus Animals' Desertion, The," 113, 119, 137-138, 139, 142, 144
"Coat, A," 23, 53, 93, 145, 146, 160
"Cold Heaven, The," 47-48, 111, 142, 159
"Collar-bone of a Hare, The," 64, 65, 68
"Coole and Ballylee, 1931," 100, 103, 105, 143
"Coole Park, 1929," 100-103, 104, 105
"Crazy Jane and the Bishop," 74, 133, 134, 155
"Crazy Jane Talks with the Bishop," 74, 86, 133, 134, 155
Crossways, 32, 33, 54
"Cuchulain's Fight with the Sea," 51, 107, 142, 147
"Death," 125-126, 147
"Dialogue of Self and Soul, A," 64, 75, 110, 113, 122, 123, 131-132, 133, 14-148, 155
"Dolls, The," 90, 92-93

"Double Vision of Michael Robartes, The," 75-76, 78, 82, 88, 95, 97, 157
"Easter, 1916," 78, 79, 80, 147, 157, 158
Essays, 15, 16, 21, 30, 120, 125, 137
Explorations, 15, 84, 161
"Fergus and the Druid," 49-50, 51
"Grey Rock, The," 89-90
"Gyres, The," 51, 98, 99, 136-137, 147, 149
"High Talk," 31, 140, 142, 143, 145, 146, 160
"His Phoenix," 75
"In Memory of Major Robert Gregory," 105-106, 107, 112, 158
"In the Seven Woods," 60
In the Seven Woods, 32
"Indian to his Love, The," 39, 40-41, 42
"Indian Upon God, The," 33, 39, 40, 42, 74
"Into the Twilight," 53
"Lake Isle of Innisfree, The," 42, 43, 86, 115, 154
"Lamentation of the Old Pensioner, The," 25, 128, 137, 147, 159
"Lapis Lazuli," 135, 136, 145, 147
"Leda and the Swan," 27-29, 69, 70, 71, 72-73, 74, 75, 82, 125, 141, 155
"Literary Movement in Ireland, The," 87
"Magi, The," 90, 91-92, 155
"Man Who Dreamed of Faeryland, The," 85
"Meditation of the Old Fisherman," 44-45
"Meru," 36, 120, 121, 127
"Michael Robartes and the Dancer," 157
"Mohini Chatterjee," 86
Mosada, 33
Mythologies, 14, 15, 84
"Nineteen Hundred and Nineteen," 111, 115, 126-127, 146
"Old Men Admiring Themselves in the Water, The," 54-55
"Old Pensioner, The," 159-160
"Prayer for My Daughter, A," 107, 112, 113, 114
"Ribh Considers Christian Love Insufficient," 134-135
Rose, The, 32, 45, 46, 159, 160
"Rose of Battle, The," 47, 48-49
"Rose of Peace, The," 47, 48
"Rose of the World, The," 47
"Running to Paradise," 57, 58, 155
"Sad Shepherd, The," 41, 42, 153
"Sailing to Byzantium," 22, 85, 86, 114, 115, 117-118, 119, 122, 131, 137, 144, 158-159, 160

"Scholars, The," 18, 90
"Second Coming, The," 77, 80-81, 91, 97, 102, 120, 125, 137, 154, 155, 157
"September 1913," 56
"Solomon and the Witch," 61, 62, 63, 64
"Solomon to Sheba," 61
"Song from 'The Player Queen,' A," 25-26
"Song of the Happy Shepherd, The," 33-36, 37, 38, 39, 41, 55, 84-85, 86, 99, 122-123, 140, 153
"Song of the Old Mother, The," 53-54
"Song of Wandering Aengus, The," 52, 154
"Statues, The," 84, 94, 99, 145
"Sweet Dancer," 88
"There," 27
"Three Beggars, The," 57, 58, 155, 158
"Three Hermits, The," 55, 155
"To Be Carved on a Stone at Thoor Ballylee," 86
"To Some I have Talked with by the Fire," 60
"To the Rose upon the Rood of Time," 45-46
"Tower, The," 107-111
"Two Songs of a Fool," 24
"Two Trees, The," 55-56, 155
"Under Ben Bulben," 139
"Vacillation," 64, 75, 132, 133
Variorum Edition of Poems, The, 17
Vision, A, 59, 91, 97, 121, 137, 143, 154, 157, 160
"What Then?" 121
"White Birds, The," 57-58, 60
"Who Goes with Fergus," 50
"Why Should Not Old Men Be Mad?" 125, 126, 128
"Wild Old Wicked Man, The," 136
"Wild Swans at Coole, The," 25, 67, 68, 74, 123-124, 127, 141
Wind Among the Reeds, The, 53, 155
"Withering of the Boughs, The," 57

Young, David, 68

Zwerdling, Alex, 32, 53, 62, 63, 90